Pedometer Power

Power

67 Lessons for K–12

Robert P. Pangrazi, PhD
Aaron Beighle, MS
Arizona State University

Cara L. Sidman, PhD
James Madison University

Human Kinetics

Library of Congress Cataloging-in-Publication Data

Pangrazi, Robert P.
   Pedometer power : 67 lessons for k-12 / Robert P. Pangrazi, Aaron
Beighle, Cara L. Sidman.
      p. cm.
Includes bibliographical references.
   ISBN 0-7360-4484-1 (pbk.)
   1. Exercise--Measurement. 2. Physical education and training. I.
Beighle, Aaron, 1972- II. Sidman, Cara L., 1972- III. Title.
   QP301 .P34 2003
   612'.04'0287--dc21

                               2002012686

ISBN: 0-7360-4484-1

The Web addresses cited in this text were current as of August 2002, unless otherwise
noted.

Acquisitions Editor: Bonnie Pettifor; **Managing Editor:** Amy Stahl; **Assistant Editor:**
Derek Campbell; **Copyeditor:** Ozzievelt Owens; **Proofreader:** Erin Cler; **Permission
Manager:** Dalene Reeder; **Graphic Designer:** Fred Starbird; **Graphic Artist:** Kathleen
Boudreau-Fuoss; **Photo Manager:** Leslie A. Woodrum; **Cover Designer:** Keith Blomberg;
Photographer (cover): Dan Wendt; **Photographer (interior):** Leslie A. Woodrum, unless
otherwise noted; **Art Manager:** Kelly Hendren; **Illustrator:** Accurate Art; **Printer:** United
Graphics

Printed in the United States of America   10   9   8   7   6   5   4   3

Human Kinetics
Web site: www.HumanKinetics.com

United States: Human Kinetics
P.O. Box 5076
Champaign, IL 61825-5076
800-747-4457
e-mail: humank@hkusa.com

Canada: Human Kinetics
475 Devonshire Road, Unit 100
Windsor, ON N8Y 2L5
800-465-7301 (in Canada only)
e-mail: orders@hkcanada.com

Europe: Human Kinetics
107 Bradford Road
Stanningley
Leeds LS28 6AT, United Kingdom
+44 (0)113 255 5665
e-mail: hk@hkeurope.com

Australia: Human Kinetics
57A Price Avenue
Lower Mitcham, South Australia 5062
08 8277 1555
e-mail: liaw@hkaustralia.com

New Zealand: Human Kinetics
Division of Sports Distributors NZ Ltd.
P.O. Box 300 226 Albany
North Shore City, Auckland
0064 9 448 1207
e-mail: blairc@hknewz.com

Contents

Chapter 4
Basic Pedometer Activities   41

Chapter 5
Pedometer Activities
for Elementary School Students   59

Chapter 6
Pedometer Activities
for Secondary School Students   91

Chapter 7
Pedometer Activities for Families   105

Preface

Welcome to the new and exciting world of pedometers. This inexpensive device gives you, the physical education teacher, a means of helping your students develop patterns of physical activity and teaching them how to monitor the amount of activity they accumulate on a daily basis. Pedometers also offer you a concise and easy way to show parents how physical education programs can increase the physical activity levels of their children. Is there a better legacy that physical education can leave students and their parents than an active lifestyle? Invariably, most people overestimate how active they are on a daily basis. With the rate of obesity increasing across the United States, a need exists for a quick and reliable way to measure physical activity. The pedometer is such a tool.

Chapter 1 of this book discusses the need for physical activity and supports the philosophy of promoting physical activity for students. This chapter provides basic information about moderate to vigorous physical activity and the benefits of such activity. It also gives information about activity guidelines for students. Chapter 2 presents different methods of measuring activity and discusses goal-setting strategies for motivating students to be more active. Goal setting is a personalized way of establishing a baseline activity level and setting an achievable target level of activity.

Chapters 3 and 4 provide the basic knowledge needed to start using pedometers in physical education and community settings. Chapter 3 discusses starting a pedometer program, including how to store, use, and put away the devices. Chapter 4 provides a set of pedometer activities that are appropriate for students of all age and grade levels. These basic activities form the foundation of the pedometer program and include calculating stride length, converting steps to miles and kilometers, and setting personal and cooperative (group) goals. Chapters 5, 6, and 7 present activities for students in both the school and the family setting, with emphasis on helping students learn about the many aspects of monitoring physical activity and on helping them develop and maintain active lifestyles.

We have experienced the excitement pedometers have created in our activity settings. We hope you find the same. Happy moving!

Acknowledgments

Writing a book is always a group endeavor and we would like to thank a number of people for their support and aid. Firstly, Bonnie Pettifor was a most supportive editor with a positive and caring demeanor. Amy Stahl and the entire production team were efficient and precise in their work and seemed to catch all the necessary details as the book was readied for publication.

We are indebted to Deb Pangrazi, supervisor of Elementary Physical Education for the Mesa, Arizona School District for reviewing and suggesting a number of the activities in the text. Many of the Mesa Elementary physical education teachers field tested our ideas and concepts and gave suggestions for their modification. We also thank Todd Keating of the Naperville, Illinois School District for his generosity in sharing many ideas and concepts related to using pedometers in physical education classes.

A special note of thanks goes out to Deb Pangrazi and Barbara Beighle for their moral support and willingness to allow us uninterrupted time for writing. It takes a team to develop a quality publication and we all appreciate our teammates.

The Need for Physical Activity

Isabella was apprehensive about her first day at her new elementary school. She was already upset because her family had to move away from all her friends; having to go to a new school made things even worse.

Isabella successfully made it through her first few classes, but when it was time for physical education, she became nervous. She had not been required to take physical education at her old school, so it would be an entirely new experience for her—an experience she wished she could avoid.

The first physical education class with Mr. Jackson was an introduction, and the students were not required to dress for it. However, Mr. Jackson explained that the class would be an active class and that proper dress was necessary for every class period.

Isabella spoke up for the first time that day. "Mr. Jackson," she said, "why do we have to be active? I never had to be active in my old school."

"Well, Isabella," replied Mr. Jackson, "physical activity has many health benefits, and learning a variety of activities and skills at a young age will help you to be active when you're my age."

"What kind of health benefits?" Tory blurted out without raising his hand.

After reminding the students to raise their hands before speaking in class, Mr. Jackson said, "Physical activity prevents lots of diseases and helps you live a longer, healthier life. But, even more important, it will make you look better and feel stronger." With that statement, the time for talking and listening ended, and the time for activity, having fun, and getting stronger began.

For over 40 years, American students were viewed as physically unfit and in need of strenuous and structured physical activity. The goal of physical educators was to push students to develop high levels of physical fitness without concern for long-term outcomes. An underlying assumption was that if we got them fit as children, they would stay fit as adults. Obviously, this assumption was incorrect, and today the United States is engaged in a battle with the bulge. In the 1990s, a new analysis of previous data (Corbin and Pangrazi 1992) showed that the fitness levels of students had not decreased and had in fact increased in some cases (with the exception of obesity). This finding brought about a shift in thinking: If fitness testing discouraged many of the students who had done poorly or failed the test, what was the point? If pushing students to be fit often backfired because those who needed it the most hated it the most, something had to change.

A new approach grew out of this new thinking—an approach that placed strong emphasis on promoting physical activity for all students regardless of natural ability and other genetic limitations. The shift from structured and often forced physical activity to lifestyle physical activity is supported by scientific studies that demonstrate benefits from moderate amounts of activity (Dunn, Andersen, and Jakicic 1998). The specific goal stated in *Healthy People 2010* to "improve health, fitness, and quality of life through daily physical activity" (USDHHS 1998) emphasizes the trend toward performing daily physical activity rather than scoring well on a physical fitness test. Obviously, lifestyle activity and fitness are related; a physically active lifestyle may ultimately lead to physical fitness. Although many uncontrollable (genetic) factors influence the extent to which a person is capable of attaining physical fitness, every child can successfully participate in physical activity.

In the past decade, research has demonstrated that virtually everyone can benefit from daily moderate to vigorous physical activity. This finding has tremendous implications for public health and quality of life. The leading cause of death in the United States is cardiovascular disease, which is preventable through healthy lifestyle choices (Corbin,

Lindsey, and Welk 2000). Educational programs that focus on healthy lifestyle choices can play an integral role in improving the health of the nation in the next decade. Specifically, increasing student participation in physical activity in the schools and promoting lifelong physical activity can help the nation reach its goals by the year 2010.

What Is Moderate to Vigorous Physical Activity?

Experts generally agree on what constitutes light, moderate, and vigorous physical activity. Resting metabolic rates (METs) are used to quantify the intensity of physical activity. One MET equals the amount of calories (energy) expended at rest (resting metabolism). Activity that expends twice as much energy equals 2 METs, activity that expends three times as much energy equals 3 METs, and so on. Activities that expend 3 METs or less are considered light activities. Examples of such activities are strolling (slow walking), slow stationary cycling, stretching, golf with a motorized cart, fishing (sitting), bowling, carpet sweeping, and riding a mower (Pate et al. 1995). Activities that expend 4 to 6 METs are considered moderate activities. Examples of moderate-level activities are brisk walking, racket sports, and mowing the lawn with a power mower. To meet the new recommendation, a person should do 30 minutes of moderate-level activity on most, if not all, days of the week.

Benefits of Moderate to Vigorous Physical Activity

Research linking physical activity to health benefits, specifically to cardiorespiratory health and fitness, provides the rationale for physical educators to promote and implement the pedometer programs and ideas outlined in this book. Two key studies that prompted the national health concern for sedentary living were based on epidemiological findings relating physical activity to a mortality reduction in men. Paffenbarger and colleagues (1986) examined more than 16,000 Harvard alumni over a span of 12 to 16 years to determine the positive relation between physical activity and longevity, and mortality reduction from all causes. Their results illustrated a clear 10 percent advantage for men expending more than 2,000 calories a week, with some benefits seen at expenditures of 500 calories a week. This dose-response relation (i.e., the amount of activity necessary to cause positive health changes) has consequently become the focus of further investigation with regard to both physical and psychological benefits.

Blair and colleagues (1995) studied approximately 10,000 healthy and unhealthy men over 5 years to determine the relation between physical fitness changes and the risk of mortality. Their results indicated that physical fitness could reduce all-cause mortality and cardiovascular disease. Although most of the pioneering epidemiological studies were based on adult men, the benefit of physical activity to health is well established for everyone.

Exercise-training studies have reported health-related benefits from moderate-intensity activities (Haskell 1994). Consistent with this idea is the promotion of activity volume (duration and frequency) rather than intensity to reach health goals. Essentially, the dose-response relation refers to the premise that benefits increase as the amount of activity increases (Haskell 1994). Because a number of studies report similar conclusions, researchers are focusing on the total amount of physical activity performed daily rather than on the intensity of the physical activity.

Additional research by Dunn and colleagues (1999) sought to investigate the specific type of physical activity needed to elicit health benefits. These researchers conducted a study to determine the effects of lifestyle activity and structured activity on subsequent physical activity level and cardiorespiratory fitness. Lifestyle activity was defined as 30 minutes or more of accumulated moderate-intensity physical activity that was part of daily routines on most or all days of the week as described in the Surgeon General's guidelines (USDHHS 1996). Structured activity involved a traditional exercise prescription, requiring an intensity of 50 to 85 percent of maximal aerobic power for 20 to 60 minutes and attendance at least three supervised workout sessions a week. After 24 months, physical activity was measured by a 7-day recall questionnaire, and cardiorespiratory fitness was measured by a maximal treadmill test. Cholesterol, blood pressure, and body composition were also included as secondary outcome measures.

Dunn et al. (1999) concluded that lifestyle activity intervention was as effective as structured activity intervention in improving physical activity and fitness levels among previously sedentary healthy adults. Therefore, the traditional structured exercise prescription recommending 20 to 60 minutes of physical activity at a specific intensity level is modifiable, depending on goals. For physical educators, if the goal is to teach students the benefits of physical activity and ultimately turn them on to a lifetime of activity participation, using lifestyle intervention (as the Surgeon General recommends) is sufficient and probably more effective than structured intervention in developing and maintaining positive attitudes.

A variety of investigators have conducted studies of the relation between the amount of activity and the subsequent benefits. Health and physical educators need this knowledge when they teach and recommend daily activities for their students. They can use it to design quality physical education programs that positively affect the health of students (Haskell 1994).

Fitness Testing and Accountability

Physical educators teach a variety of students with widely varying physical capabilities. Educators must take into account the different skill and fitness levels of their students and how these differences are influenced by heredity. The role of heredity in determining physical fitness abilities is well documented (Bouchard 1999). For example, only a small percentage of students have the genetic predisposition to perform the optimal number of pull-ups to place them in the high-fitness zone on fitness tests. However, all students can be physically active when walking or performing other locomotor movements. Because high-fitness performance is impossible for the vast majority of students, emphasis should be placed on lifestyle physical activity. Lifestyle activity can be performed by all students regardless of their physical limitations. Successful lifestyle experiences in a "can do" environment increase the chance of students maturing into active adults.

Despite this new information and knowledge, many physical education programs continue to promote physical fitness outcomes rather than lifestyle physical activity. Physical fitness tests remain the most common form of evaluation in physical education (Hopple and Graham 1995). Beighle, Pangrazi, and Vincent (2001) proposed that evaluation of students should focus on identifying those who are physically inactive. The focus on fitness goals does little to help identify students who are inactive.

If students with a genetic predisposition are able to achieve high fitness scores without accumulating adequate amounts of daily physical activity, they may leave school believing they can be physically fit without being active. Similarly, students who are physically active and spend a lot of time training may still score poorly on a fitness test because of their genetic limitations. This poor performance creates disappointment and might lead to a "what's the use of trying" attitude.

Essentially, the role of fitness testing for accountability in physical education should be rethought. Teaching students to personally evaluate their own fitness levels as they participate in self-testing activities is positive and helpful. However, using fitness tests for grading or evaluating the success of a physical education program can be counterproductive.

Authentic evaluation of daily physical activity that identifies inactive students and rewards those who become more active will create good will among students, parents, teachers, and administrators. What school administrators wouldn't want to graduate students who have a positive attitude toward physical activity and know how to evaluate their personal levels of activity? What parents wouldn't appreciate teachers who help their children develop and maintain a healthy lifestyle?

This book facilitates this accountability shift to daily physical activity through the use of the digital pedometer, a small instrument that attaches to the waistband and measures footsteps. Pedometers can be used to evaluate students' level of activity and teach them to be active in a low-cost, accurate, and private manner. For a student who dislikes physical activity, the pedometer can bring about positive changes in attitude and behavior. The pedometer is easy to use, unthreatening, personal (no one has to see how many steps a student has taken), and able to gather physical activity data throughout the waking hours.

Physical Activity for Students

Sallis and McKenzie (1991) presented an in-depth discussion of the benefits of physical activity and the role of physical education. Elementary schools are important sites for promoting regular physical activity because of their potential influence on students. Sallis and McKenzie (1991) reported that up to 97 percent of elementary school students participate in some type of physical education program, thus highlighting the role such programs can play in health and fitness. Rationales for changing physical education programs to increase daily physical activity participation are based on sound epidemiological and empirical findings. Teaching the importance and enjoyment of physical activity to students can create health behavior patterns that carry over from childhood into adulthood.

Daily physical activity produces benefits that affect healthy growth and development. For example, physical activity at an early age improves peak bone density during critical growth periods (Sallis and McKenzie 1991). In a study by Bailey and colleagues (1995), bouts of intermittent physical activity (alternating periods of vigorous activity and rest) were shown to stimulate the release of growth hormone. This pattern of activity is typical of students and appears to be necessary to ensure optimal growth.

Physical Activity Guidelines for Students

When developing and revising physical education curriculums, instructors should consider the Surgeon General's lifetime activity guidelines and the unique physical activity needs of students (Pangrazi, Corbin, and Welk 1996). Whereas adults struggle to incorporate physical activity into their daily routines, children are inherently active throughout the day.

Guidelines for Preadolescents

Preadolescent children are not miniature adults; therefore, physical activity recommendations for preadolescents must reflect their unique characteristics and needs. Pangrazi, Corbin, and Welk (1996) identify distinct behavior differences between adults and children and make sound recommendations based on these differences. Children have the ability to accumulate a greater volume of physical activity than adults, mostly because of the greater amount of discretionary time they have available. They resist high-intensity activities and prefer relatively large amounts of moderate-intensity activities. In addition, children are sporadic in their physical activity participation, alternating bouts of activity with bouts of recovery (which stimulates the release of growth hormone). As a result of these findings, Corbin, Pangrazi, and Welk (1994) specify that total volume is a good indicator of childhood activity, which educators must consider when implementing and evaluating physical education programs in the schools. Thus, measuring students' accumulated physical activity throughout the day using pedometers is a way to assess progression toward health goals.

Guidelines for Adolescents

A board of experts has developed a consensus statement that recommends the amount of activity adolescents should have on a regular basis. This statement delineates the amount of activity adolescents ages 11 to 21 need and contains two basic guidelines (Sallis and Patrick 1994). **Guideline 1** states that "All adolescents should be physically active daily, or nearly every day, as part of play, games, sports, work, transportation, recreation, physical education, or planned exercise, in the context of family, school, and community activities" (p. 307). Adolescents who participate in 30 minutes of activity meet the first guideline. **Guideline 2** states that "Adolescents should engage in three or more sessions per week of activities that last 20 minutes or more and require moderate to vigorous levels of exertion" (p. 308).

Meeting guideline 1 should be a priority and a minimum goal for students. Participation in 30 minutes of daily activity is a reasonable goal, even for sedentary students. Beyond the minimum, meeting guideline 2 is a desirable goal. The consensus statement suggests brisk walking, jogging, stair climbing, basketball, racket sports, soccer, dance, swimming laps, skating, strength training (resistance training), lawn mowing, and cycling as activities that meet guideline 2. Maintaining the heart rate at a

Active and sedentary students.

preselected target for the full 20 minutes is not necessary for meeting guideline 2, and many of the activities listed do not produce such a result.

Because benefits can be realized at moderate levels of physical activity and students inherently select moderate intensities, it seems appropriate to motivate students to perform activities they enjoy and can easily sustain for a lifetime. If this concept of promoting lifestyle activity can be applied to physical education, the health of the nation can be significantly improved. As stated in *Healthy People 2010*, "Because children spend most of their time in school, the type and amount of physical activity encouraged in schools are important components of a fitness program and a healthy lifestyle" (USDHHS 1998).

If You Want to Know More . . .

The following sections are helpful if you want to know more about topics in this chapter. The Web sites contain information that is constantly updated and revised. Many of the government Web sites are useful because they contain current survey data and information for improving the health of youth.

Web Sites

www.health.gov/healthypeople
The Web site for *Healthy People 2010*.

www.cdc.gov
The Web site of the Centers for Disease Control and Prevention.

http://pe.central.vt.edu/index.html
PE Central is a Web site for health and physical education teachers.

www.cdc.gov/nccdphp/dash/cshpdef.htm
A Coordinated School Health Program—The Centers for Disease Control's eight-component model of school health programs.

www.pe4life.com
P.E.4Life: Active Body, Active Mind. This Web site promotes quality physical education programs for America's youth.

www.cdc.gov/nccdphp/sgr/adoles.htm
Physical Activity and Health: A Report of the Surgeon General—Adolescents and Young Adults.

www.cdc.gov/nccdphp/dash/presphysactrpt
Adolescent and School Health—Promoting Better Health for Young People Through Physical Activity and Sports.

www.pecentral.org/professional/pepbill/pepmoney.html
This Web site provides a Physical Education for Progress (PEP) bill update, a grant program passed in 2002 to provide funding to help communities create innovative physical education programs in the schools (includes hiring and training teachers and purchasing new equipment).

References

Bailey, R.C., J. Olson, S.L. Pepper, J. Porszaz, T.J. Barstow, and D.M. Cooper. 1995. The level and tempo of children's physical activities: An observational study. *Med. Sci. Sport Exer.* 27:1033–41.

Beighle, A., R.P. Pangrazi, and S.D. Vincent. 2001. Pedometers, physical activity, and accountability. *JOPERD* 72:16–36.

Blair, S.N., H.W. Kohl, C.E. Barlow, R.S. Paffenbarger, L.W. Gibbons, and C.A. Macera. 1995. Changes in physical fitness and all-cause mortality: A prospective study of healthy and unhealthy men. *JAMA* 273:1093–98.

Bouchard, C. 1999. Heredity and health related fitness. In *Toward a better understanding of physical fitness and activity*, ed. C.B. Corbin and R.P. Pangrazi, 11–17. Scottsdale, AZ: Holcomb Hathaway Publishers.

Corbin, C.B., R. Lindsey, and G. Welk. 2000. *Concepts of fitness and wellness: A comprehensive lifestyle approach* (3rd ed). Boston: McGraw-Hill.

Corbin, C.B., and R.P. Pangrazi. 1992. Are American children and youth fit? *Res. Q. Exercise Sport* 63:96–106.

Corbin, C.B., R.P. Pangrazi, and G.J. Welk. 1994. Toward an understanding of appropriate physical activity levels for youth. *Physical Activity and Fitness Research Digest* 1:1–8.

Dunn, A.L., R.E. Andersen, and J.M. Jakicic. 1998. Lifestyle physical activity interventions. *Am. J. Prev. Med.* 15:398–412.

Dunn, A.L., B.H. Marcus, J.B. Kampert, M.E. Garcia, H.W. Kohl, and S.N. Blair. 1999. Comparison of lifestyle and structured interventions to increase physical activity and cardiorespiratory fitness: A randomized trial. *JAMA* 281:327–34.

Haskell, W.L. 1994. Health consequences of physical activity: Understanding and challenges regarding dose-response. *Med. Sci. Sport Exer.* 26:649–60.

Hopple, C., and G. Graham. 1995. What children think, feel, and know about physical fitness testing. *JTPE* 14:408–17.

Paffenbarger, R.S., R.T. Hyde, A.L. Wing, and C.C. Hsieh. 1986. Physical activity, all-cause mortality, and longevity of college alumni. *New Engl. J. Med.* 314:605–13.

Pangrazi, R.P., C.B. Corbin, and G.J. Welk. 1996. Physical activity for children and youth. *JOPERD* 67:38–43.

Pate, R., M. Pratt, S. Blair, W. Haskell, C. Macera, C. Bouchard, D. Buchner, W. Ettinger, G. Heath, A. King, A. Kriska, A. Leon, B. Marcus, J. Morris, R. Paffenbarger, K. Patrick, M. Pollock, J. Rippe, J. Sallis, and J. Wilmore. 1995. Physical activity and public health. *JAMA* 273:402–7.

Sallis, J.F., and T.L. McKenzie. 1991. Physical education's role in public health. *Res. Q. Exercise Sport* 62:124–37.

Sallis, J.F., and K. Patrick. 1994. Physical activity guidelines for adolescents: Consensus statement. *Pediatr. Exerc. Sci.* 6:302–14.

U.S. Department of Health and Human Services (USDHHS). 1998. Physical activity and fitness. In *Healthy People 2010 Objectives: Part B, Focus Area 22*. **www.health.gov/healthypeople**.

U.S. Department of Health and Human Services (USDHHS). 1996. *Physical activity and health: A report of the Surgeon General.* Atlanta: Centers for Disease Control and Prevention, and National Center for Chronic Disease Prevention and Health Promotion.

Physical Activity Measurement and Goal Setting

"**W**hat's that on your belt, Miss Tanaka?" asked Jessica when her physical education teacher walked into the gym to start class.

"Well, Jessica," replied Miss Tanaka, "it's a pedometer, and it's used to measure how many steps I take throughout the day."

"Why would you want to know how many steps you take in a day?" Jessica asked.

"That's what we're going to talk about today, so I'm glad you asked!" exclaimed Miss Tanaka, and she began the lesson about physical activity and the use of pedometers.

By wearing a pedometer to class, Miss Tanaka was able to create interest in it. Once Jessica started asking about the device, the rest of the class became involved. They listened to the conversation between Jessica and Miss Tanaka and asked additional questions themselves—exactly what Miss Tanaka had hoped would happen.

Miss Tanaka started her pedometer lesson with a brief discussion of the device. After the initial discussion, she gave each student a pedometer and allowed the students to become familiar with them. She explained how pedometers work and what they measure. Then she asked the students a question: "How many steps does it take to walk from your house to school?" No one had any idea. Miss Tanaka asked another question: "How many steps do you take each school day?" Again, no one really knew, but now they couldn't wait to use their pedometers to find out.

Chapter 2 discusses a number of ways that physical activity can be measured. The pedometer will be emphasized as the measurement device of choice for most teachers because it is inexpensive and easy to interpret. A second focal point of the chapter is goal setting. Teaching students to measure and evaluate their baseline activity level is presented as an important part of a successful goal-setting strategy.

Measuring Physical Activity

Measuring physical activity is important for people of all ages. Often, when adults are asked if they are active, they respond with a resounding "Yes!" However, without actually measuring their physical activity, people don't really know their activity level or understand their activity needs. One reason to measure the activity levels of students is to give them an understanding of the importance of physical activity that they will carry into adulthood.

How active are your students? How much activity do they accumulate during the school day? How much activity do they accumulate outside of the school setting? All physical activity accumulated throughout the day has health benefits for students. The challenge is to know how to measure the accumulated activity. Measurement of physical activity can serve not only to assess physical activity levels but also to show the importance of an active lifestyle. The knowledge that students gain about their personal physical activity levels may motivate them to alter their physical activity patterns.

Measuring physical activity also gives physical education teachers a way to evaluate the effectiveness of their programs. A program designed to promote physical activity should result in higher physical activity levels. Valid physical activity measurements will allow teachers to determine whether their programs are effective. Evaluating physical activity requires an assessment tool that must travel with the student throughout the day. The tool must not only be mobile but also have the capability to record data manually or electronically.

Measurement of physical activity for a single day is not sufficient to accurately capture the physical activity patterns of students. Data must be taken over a period of 4 days (for elementary school students) to 8 days (for middle/high school students). Students can either manually record the data each day or use an instrument that is capable of storing the information.

Several techniques and tools are currently used to measure physical activity, including

- self-monitoring,
- self-report questionnaires,
- direct observation,
- heart rate monitors,
- accelerometers, and
- pedometers.

Self-monitoring and self-report questionnaires are similar, subjective measures that rely on accounting of physical activity by the students. Self-monitoring and self-report instruments must also be validated for accuracy.

The remaining tools are objective measures that assess actual movement or physiological responses while students are engaged in physical activity. Tables 2.1 and 2.2 describe the most common physical activity measurement methods and the advantages and disadvantages of each.

Pedometers

Pedometers have been used for centuries (they were said to be invented by Leonardo da Vinci) as people have tried to measure distances they traveled while walking. Because early mechanical pedometers were not highly accurate, researchers were hesitant to use them to evaluate physical activity levels. Electronic pedometers are much more sensitive and accurate than nonelectronic models in delivering step counts and are now used in many studies to measure walking-related activity. Electronic pedometers detect movement through a spring-loaded, counterbalanced mechanism that records vertical acceleration at the hip. Compared with other currently used assessment tools, such as self-report questionnaires or diaries, pedometers are now an acceptable method of objectively measuring total daily step counts.

Pedometers measure the up-and-down motion of the hip in a vertical plane. Numerous studies have examined the validity of pedometers and have concluded that the device is a suitable tool for assessing the physical activity patterns of students (Welk et al. 2000).

Pedometers have limitations. They cannot measure frequency or intensity of physical activity. They simply assess the total number of steps performed

Table 2.1   Methods of Measuring Physical Activity

Method	Description
Direct observation	Trained observers follow participants for the entire measurement period while time-sampling physical activity. Time-sampling involves documenting physical activity for a specific time period (e.g., 1 minute) followed by a short break (e.g., 20 seconds).
Self-report	Participants document their activity level at the same time each day. Each morning they log their activity for the previous day. Some instruments collect data for 2 days; others collect for as many as 7 days.
Heart rate monitors	Heart rate monitors indirectly assess physical activity by measuring the heart's response to physical activity. Heart rate increases with increases in the intensity of physical activity.
Uniaxial accelerometers	Uniaxial accelerometers generally measure body movement (usually at the hip) in the vertical plane. This movement is best thought of as an up-and-down motion. They are much more costly and larger in size than pedometers. They can record and print out a record of all movements by time of day.
Triaxial accelerometers	Triaxial accelerometers assess physical activity by measuring movement in three planes: side-to-side, vertical, and horizontal.

Table 2.2   Advantages and Disadvantages of Physical Activity Measuring Methods

Method	Advantage	Disadvantage
Direct observation	Direct measurements	Time requirements Difficult to use with large populations Obtrusive
Self-report	Ease of administration with large populations Cost effective	Difficult for children because of the cognitive requirements Subject bias
Heart rate monitors	Direct relationship between heart rate and energy expenditure Can estimate energy expenditure Travel unobtrusively with the user	Influenced by many factors, such as age, emotional stress, and fitness level Heart rate changes slowly relative to changes in physical activity, potentially disguising the sporadic nature of children's movements

(continued)

Method	Advantage	Disadvantage
Accelerometers	Store data, permitting the assessment of the frequency, intensity, and duration of physical activity Provide data at specific times of the day to assess physical activity patterns Detect the intermittent activity of children Unobtrusive	May not measure some forms of activity (e.g., cycling and stair climbing) Costly

Reprinted, by permission, from A. Beighle, R.P. Pangrazi, and S.D. Vincent, 2001, "Pedometers, physical activity, and accountability," *JOPERD* 72 (9):18.

Students using pedometers in a physical education class.
Photo courtesy of Walk4Life, Inc.

in a day. However, for physical education teachers who want an inexpensive and easy-to-maintain measuring tool, the limitations of the pedometer appear to be acceptable for the physical education activities proposed in this book. It is a valid, reliable, and unobtrusive instrument, and when all factors are considered, it is most suited for physical educators.

The usefulness of pedometers for measuring physical activity among students and for evaluating physical education programs is widely accepted (Beighle, Pangrazi, and Vincent 2001). Consequently, this device has become widely used for assessing total physical activity in a variety of populations. It can help bridge the gap between science and practice by providing a means of applying lifetime activity guidelines to the physical education curriculum.

Daily Pedometer Step Goals

A primary use of pedometers in physical education is to help students monitor their daily activity and set meaningful goals. You should guide students in establishing individual step goals that will take them to a healthy level of activity. Incorporate their personal goals into lesson plans, and use incentives to promote active lifestyle choices and behaviors. See chapters 5 and 6 for lesson ideas.

Baseline Activity Levels and Personal Goals

The 10,000-step physical activity target goal has received widespread attention since its initial introduction as a business slogan in Japan (Hatano 1993). Yamanouchi, Shinozaki, and Chikada (1995) suggested that the accumulation of 10,000 steps throughout the day was equivalent to meeting national health recommendations for adults. However, little research has been conducted to see whether this goal is good for all adults. Welk et al. (2000) provided empirical evidence for a 10,000-step goal for adults, but they gave little consideration to the participants' baseline activity levels. In other words, is one goal good for everyone, regardless of body type, age, sex, or genetic endowment? A better approach may be to first determine individual activity levels and then set goals from those points. These **baseline activity levels** will vary among people in a similar age range. Obviously, not all students are capable of running at the same speed, or jumping the same height, or throwing a ball with the same velocity. Therefore, try to set daily student activity goals based on their baseline activity levels.

A study of adult sedentary women (Wilde, Sidman, and Corbin 2001) showed how much baseline activity levels could vary in groups that appear similar. Daily step counts from regular daily activities ranged from 2,000 to 5,000 steps in the study group consisting of women with similar low-activity jobs (i.e., administrative assistants). This result demonstrates that a single goal, such as 10,000 steps, is not appropriate for everyone.

Goal Setting

Pedometers make setting goals for students simple because the data are objective and easy for students to understand. Learning to set specific, realistic, yet challenging goals leads students to higher levels of performance (Hall and Kerr 2001). Three factors that will help students establish goals that promote lifestyle change are

1. high ability,
2. high commitment to the goal, and
3. feedback related to goal progress.

These factors will optimize personal growth and change in both physical education and sport settings. Teachers can have an impact on only one of the three factors—the feedback issue. Because pedometers offer instant feedback to students, the teacher's role becomes that of a facilitator who answers such questions as the following:

- What does my number of steps mean?
- Do I need to accumulate more steps every day?
- How many steps should I increase as part of my new goal?
- How many steps are enough for good health?

Answers to these questions become part of the feedback that students can learn to interpret. Feedback is one of the most important aspects of the physical education of students. It plays a vital role in helping students learn how to structure and develop meaningful outcomes and in achieving desired goals.

Individual Goals

Different types of goals can help students modify and increase their activity behavior. Individual goals allow students to work independently. This text advocates individual goals for designing a program of personal development. Individual goals are not used for evaluative or comparative purposes for anyone other than the student for whom they were designed to motivate. Individual goals are ideal for promoting lifestyle activity and encouraging self-improvement. They teach students self-direction because there is no peer interaction or adult supervision. Rather, each student assumes the responsibility for self-improvement. Students who reach their individual goals may feel increased motivation and higher self-esteem, and they may develop a sense of self-efficacy (the belief that one is capable of performing a specific behavior).

Cooperative Goals

Cooperative goals require students to work together to achieve desired outcomes. All students within the group are expected to contribute to accomplishing the goals. The goals can build group cohesiveness if all students feel that they can contribute. Cooperative goal setting is appropriate when the goal is to increase positive social interaction behaviors. They can enhance self-esteem because they make participation by each member of the group necessary for the success of the entire group. Because each student is an important part of the group, they will often encourage and help one another reach the desired outcome. The use of cooperative goals can only be effective if desired outcomes are achievable for all participating students. Achieving a specific pedometer step count is a cooperative goal that every student who is able to walk can accomplish. If students with disabilities are participating with the class, they should have modified goals that allow them to contribute to the desired outcome.

Competitive Goals

Competitive goals are designed to pit individual students or groups of students against each other. A competitive objective is achievable by only one student or group of students. Competitive goal structuring is best used after students have acquired and overlearned motor and cognitive skills. Because the majority of elementary school students have not overlearned skills, competitive goals are probably not a good choice. However, for high school students, competitively structured goals can increase performance.

In summary, teachers play a critical role in developing and implementing goals for their students. Usually, the safest and most effective goals are those that are personal and individual.

If You Want to Know More . . .

This section offers information for finding pedometers and related materials to help in designing a quality activity program for students. Many of the articles discuss the effectiveness of pedometers as a tool for promoting physical activity among youth of all ages.

Web Sites

www.cdc.gov/nccdphp/sgr/chap2.htm
Physical Activity and Health. A Report of the Surgeon General: Chapter 2 —Historical Background, Terminology, Evolution of Recommendations, and Measurement.

www.indiana.edu/~preschal/index.shtml
The President's Challenge: Physical Activity and Fitness Awards Program.

www.fitness.gov
A site developed by the President's Council on Physical Fitness and Sports (PCPFS). This site includes information and guidelines for the Presidential Physical Fitness Award Program, which is designed to help physical educators encourage children and adolescents 6 to 17 years of age make a commitment to increased physical activity and a lifetime of fitness.

www.walk4life.com
A Web site that provides a catalog of pedometers, PE teacher kits, pedometer tips, and accessories.

www.HumanKinetics.com
Human Kinetics home page. This site provides a reference list of books regarding physical activity measurement as well as many other physical education, health, fitness, dance, and recreation topics.

Books

Deci, E.L. and R.M. Ryan. 1985. *Intrinsic motivation and self-determination in human behavior.* New York: Plenum.

Pangrazi, R.P. 2001. *Dynamic physical education for elementary school children (13th ed.).* Boston: Allyn & Bacon.

Articles

Bailey, R.C., J. Olson, S.L. Pepper, J. Porszaz, T.J. Barstow, and D.M. Cooper. 1995. The level and tempo of children's physical activities: An observational study. *Med. Sci. Sport Exer.* 27:1033–41.

Corbin, C.B. and R.P. Pangrazi. 1992. Are American children and youth fit? *Res. Q. Exercise Sport* 63:96–106.

Dunn, A.L., R.E. Andersen, and J.M. Jakicic. 1998. Lifestyle physical activity interventions. *Am. J. Preventive Med.* 15:398–412.

Sallis, J.F. and T.L. McKenzie. 1991. Physical education's role in public health. *Res. Q. Exercise Sport* 62:124–37.

References

Beighle, A., R.P. Pangrazi, and S.D. Vincent. 2001. Pedometers, physical activity, and accountability. *JOPERD* 72:16–36.

Hall, H.K. and A.W. Kerr. 2001. Goal setting in sport and physical activity: Tracing empirical developments and establishing a conceptual direction. In *Advances in motivation in sport and exercise*, ed. G.C. Roberts, 183–233. Champaign, IL: Human Kinetics.

Hatano, Y. 1993. Use of the pedometer for promoting daily walking exercise. *International Council for Health, Physical Education and Recreation* 29:4–28.

Trost, S.G. 2001. Objective measurement of physical activity in youth: Current issues, future directions. *Exercises and Sport Sciences Reviews* 29:32–36.

Welk, G.J., F.A. Differding, R.W. Thompson, S.N. Blair, J. Dziura, and P. Hart. 2000. The utility of the Digi-Walker step counter to assess daily physical activity patterns. *Med. Sci. Sport Exerc.* 32:S481–488.

Wilde, B.E., C.L. Sidman, and C.B. Corbin. 2001. A 10,000-step count as a physical activity target for sedentary women. *Res. Q. Exercise Sport* 72:411–14.

Yamanouchi, K., K. Shinozaki, and K. Chikada. 1995. Daily walking combined with diet therapy is a useful means for obese NIDDM patients not only to reduce body weight but also to improve insulin sensitivity. *Diabetes Care* 18:775–78.

Getting Started

On Monday morning, Mr. Fina, the principal at Franklin-Monroe Elementary School, approaches the school's physical education teacher and the following conversation takes place.

Mr. Fina: Good morning, Mrs. Pankowski. I hope you had a great weekend. I have a project I'd like you to head up. Over the weekend, I read an article about using pedometers in schools. Are you familiar with them?

Mrs. Pankowski: I've read about other schools using them. Apparently they're quite effective in getting kids to become active.

Mr. Fina: Could you check into them? I think they'd fit in well with the district's new focus on incorporating technology into the curriculum. Information about their usefulness, cost, brands, and upkeep would be great to get us started.

Mrs. Pankowski: I'll do some research this week.

Mr. Fina: Oh, and the budget is tight right now, so could you also check into sources of funding?

Previous chapters have provided references and information justifying an emphasis on physical activity and the use of pedometers to assess physical activity. This chapter addresses issues such as those facing Mrs.

Pankowski by providing the information necessary to efficiently introduce pedometers into the school setting. Ideas for generating funds for pedometers, making an educated purchase, and issues specific to pedometer use with students will be discussed, as well as general uses of pedometers in the schools.

Keep in mind that assessing the effectiveness of physical activity involves student learning, not simply an evaluation of activity. Pedometers can be used to educate students about the importance of lifestyle physical activity as well as enhance the quality of a physical education program. Ideas for improving instruction, identifying at-risk students, and teaching students to use pedometers to monitor their physical activity are recurring themes in this text.

Using Pedometers in a School Setting

There are several issues to consider regarding the use of pedometers in a school setting, including

- introducing pedometers to the school,
- minimizing loss and damage,
- getting parents involved,
- distributing pedometers, and
- establishing rules for pedometer use and data recording.

The following suggestions are suitable for any level of education, up to and including the postsecondary level.

Introducing Pedometers to Students

Most likely, physical education teachers will be responsible for the pedometers and will introduce them to the students. A good place to start is with classes that are most able to quickly adapt to new ideas. Such a class offers an opportunity to test and refine the process and to work out the bugs before presenting pedometers to other classes. When students are first introduced to the pedometer, they learn what it is, how it works, and how to wear it. They then use it during a physical education class. As with all new gadgets, students will be distracted during the first few uses. Those initial lessons provide students with a chance to become accustomed to the device.

When developing a lesson plan for introducing pedometers, do the following:

1. Establish guidelines for use. Some students may shake the pedometer to artificially increase step counts. A consequence is needed to pre-

vent this behavior. "You shake it, we take it" (i.e., loss of the privilege of using the pedometer) is an effective deterrent.

2. Discuss how pedometers work, including why they are suitable for physical education. To hold the interest of the students, keep the introduction short, about 2 to 3 minutes. If necessary, break up a long discussion by allowing the students to try the pedometers and come back later for more instruction.

3. After the brief discussion, distribute the pedometers to the class. Encourage the students, under supervision only, to satisfy their curiosity about the pedometers. Let the students open the devices, shake them, reset them, and listen to them.

4. Teach students how to wear the pedometers. Pedometers are worn on the waistband directly above the knee (see figure 3.1). You should provide belts to students who wear dresses, overalls, or other types of

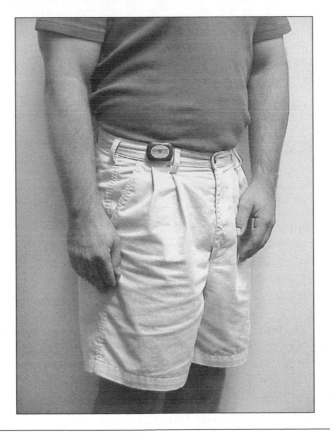

Figure 3.1   The correct placement of the pedometer is on the waistband directly above the knee.
Photo courtesy of Walk4Life, Inc.

Introducing Pedometers to a Class
- Physical activity is Important, but how do you know if you are active enough?
- Pedometers are small devices that measure steps or physical activity.
- Attach the pedometer to your waistband or belt directly above the knee. Make sure it is closed.
- Set the rule, "You shake it, I take it." (Explain that shaking destroys the accuracy of pedometers.)
- Reinforce the importance of honesty, respect, and cooperation when using pedometers. Remind students that using pedometers is a privilege that can be revoked for bad behavior.

After Pedometers Have Been Given to Students
- Under your supervision, allow students to shake the pedometers to observe the numbers increasing, and then reset the pedometer.
- Demonstrate correct placement and allow students to practice putting the pedometers on.
- Discuss belts for students without waistbands.
- Have students reset the pedometers and walk in the teaching area, periodically checking the pedometers.
- Allow students to participate in teacher-directed activities while checking the pedometers from time to time.
- Assure students that step counts are private and do not have to be shared with classmates.
- Explain that the retrieval/return system will require several practice opportunities for children to become efficient with the routine.

Figure 3.2   Instruction points for introducing pedometers.

beltless garments. Nylon belts similar to the type used for football flags work very well and are easy to make.

5. Once the students have the pedometers properly attached to their waists, have them walk inside the teaching area.

6. Finally, have the students engage in a few teacher-directed games while wearing the pedometers. While participating in activities, students periodically read the pedometers to determine their activity levels. Let the students know that their pedometer steps are private and personal, and they have no obligation to share their step counts with their peers. Figure 3.2 offers some discussion points to cover when introducing pedometers to a class.

Developing Routines for Pedometer Use

A distribution and return system will minimize disruption and decrease the amount of time necessary for retrieving and returning pedometers.

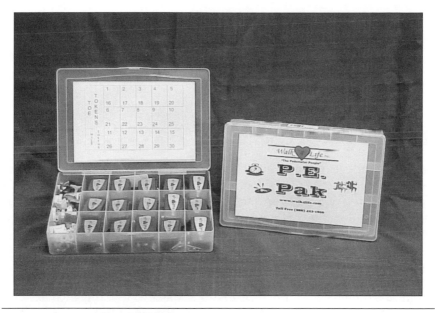

Figure 3.3 Pedometer plastic storage box.
Photo courtesy of Walk4Life, Inc.

A systematic approach also helps to minimize pedometer loss. Assign each student a pedometer that has been labeled with an identifying number. Students use only their assigned pedometers during physical education class. Students in other physical education classes are assigned these same pedometers. Therefore, you must devise a method for holding and storing the pedometers, which makes it easy to see if any are missing. See figure 3.3 for an example of pedometer storage. Other examples for pedometer storage include a hanging shoe holder, a hanging jewelry holder, a divided bucket, and a grid shoe holder. The following steps are needed for an efficient distribution and return system.

1. Keep a master list of which pedometer is assigned to which student.

2. Designate a retrieval area for the pedometers. This can be on a stage, around the perimeter of the teaching area, or in a storage device. Use the same area each lesson, and place the pedometers in the same sequence to expedite distribution and return.

3. Once students have entered the teaching area, instruct them to get their pedometers and correctly clip them in place (this can be done by squads). Students without a belt or waistband should first put on a nylon belt and fasten the pedometer to it. Ask all students to reset their pedometers to zero after they have been correctly clipped in place.

4. At the conclusion of class, instruct the students to return the pedometers to exactly where they got them.

5. Before the class leaves, check quickly for missing or damaged pedometers. This check must be done after each class. If pedometers are missing or damaged, the master list will identify the responsible students.

Recording Step Counts

Once the students become comfortable with their pedometers, they can begin recording step counts. Recording step counts teaches students to track their step counts over time. Tracking physical activity levels during physical education classes will benefit both students and the teacher. Recording physical activity levels exposes students to their own physical activity level and allows them to set goals and track their progress, as well as helps them determine what activities are the most active. Teachers can use recorded data to enhance teaching, evaluate activities, and diagnose students that are at-risk with respect to low physical activity levels. Specific activities and applications involving the use of pedometer data are covered in later chapters.

The following is a list of steps for efficiently implementing pedometer data recording by students.

1. Develop physical education step-count cards. A card can be created for each student or each pedometer. See forms 3.1 and 3.2 for examples.

2. Place a step-count card with each pedometer. If pedometers are distributed around the perimeter of the teaching area, they can be placed on the card. If a hanging holder or shoe organizer is used, the card and a pencil can be placed in the pocket with the pedometer.

3. Students returning pedometers should take the cards, open their pedometers, record their step counts on the cards, and replace the cards. This procedure should allow all students to record data privately, without the potential embarrassment of other students seeing their data.

4. Check for missing and damaged pedometers, and, if a card is made for each student, collect the cards from the students. If each student has a separate card, data collection will require teachers to quickly collect the cards from the current class and prepare the cards for the next class. Therefore, implement the data collection procedure one class at a time and become proficient with the procedure before using it with several classes.

Individual Physical Education Step-Count Record

Initials _____   Pedometer Number _____   Teacher _____

Date	Steps

Date	Steps

Date	Steps

From *Pedometer Power: 67 Lessons for K–12* by Robert P. Pangrazi, Aaron Beighle, and Cara L. Sidman, 2003, Champaign, IL: Human Kinetics.

Form 3.2

Physical Education Class Step-Count Record

Pedometer Number _____

Teacher	Day 1	Day 2	Day 3	Day 4	Day 5

From *Pedometer Power: 67 Lessons for K–12* by Robert P. Pangrazi, Aaron Beighle, and Cara L. Sidman, 2003, Champaign, IL: Human Kinetics.

Checking Out Pedometers

A long-term goal of pedometer use in any school is to have the entire school community—teachers, staff, and families—involved. To accomplish this goal, program administrators must allow pedometers to be taken out of the confines of the physical education class. Pedometers can be worn before school, during school, and after school. They also can be taken home to share with family members. However, allowing pedometers to be used outside the school opens the door to loss and damage. A checkout system is necessary that will allow pedometers to be tracked so that the number lost, damaged, or stolen is minimized.

The pedometer checkout system involves at least two situations: checking out a pedometer during the school day and checking out a pedometer to take home. Both of these situations require adult supervision and the establishment of a designated pedometer checkout area (e.g., the physical education office). Beyond these two situations, individual schools may need additional procedures for tracking pedometers.

Checking Out a Pedometer for the School Day

The following steps provide suggestions for developing a pedometer checkout system.

1. Create a short-term pedometer checkout form (STPCO) (see form 3.3).

2. Designate an area in the school where students go to check pedometers out. The physical education office or the media center is a good choice.

3. For each time period students have to check pedometers out (i.e., before school, during lunch, and after school), create a new STPCO that accompanies the pedometers, or you can include time periods together on one STPCO, as in form 3.3. If the same pedometer is checked out by different students before school and after school, a new sheet for each time period will eliminate confusion.

4. After each checkout time, inventory the pedometers, and question responsible students about any missing, lost, or damaged pedometers.

5. Keep all checkout sheets on file, particularly if there are not enough pedometers for all the students who wish to check them out. Filed checkout sheets can then be used to ensure that all students have equal opportunities to use the pedometers. A rotation by grade can assure equitable distribution of pedometers to all students.

If another adult (e.g., an aide or the media specialist) will be monitoring pedometer checkout, familiarize this person with the procedure.

Pedometer Checkout Form

Date _____

Ped. #	Morning			Lunch			After School		
	Student		Staff Initials In/Out	Student		Staff Initials In/Out	Student		Staff Initials In/Out
1									
2									
3									
4									
5									
6									
7									
8									
9									
10									
11									
12									
13									
14									
15									
16									
17									
18									
19									
20									
21									
22									
23									
24									
25									
26									
27									
28									
29									
30									
31									

From *Pedometer Power: 67 Lessons for K–12* by Robert P. Pangrazi, Aaron Beighle, and Cara L. Sidman, 2003, Champaign, IL: Human Kinetics.

Responsible students can help with the checkout procedure; however, the presence of an adult is essential, especially in the initial phases.

Checking Out a Pedometer to Take Home

Allowing students to take pedometers home can have positive consequences. The family environment is an important factor in a student's decision to be physically active (Brustad 1993, 1996; Kimiecik and Horn 1998; Freedson and Evenson 1991). Exposure to pedometers can potentially get the whole family involved in lifestyle physical activity. However, along with these potentially positive developments comes the challenge of preventing loss of pedometers. Allowing students to take pedometers home necessitates careful monitoring to minimize loss. One way to minimize loss is to limit the amount of time pedometers can be checked out to one night or one weekend. The teacher or person responsible for the pedometers should be the only person to check out pedometers to students for long-term use (i.e., overnight or for a weekend). Pedometers should not be taken home without a parent's or guardian's prior knowledge. Create a permission slip that the student's parent or guardian signs. The permission slip should include the following:

- A paragraph about pedometers that explains why the student will be bringing one home and that encourages the parents to talk to the student about physical activity.
- A paragraph explaining how to care for the pedometer.
- A statement holding the parent or student financially accountable if the pedometer is not returned or is damaged beyond the normally expected scratches or cracks. Extensive damage to the case or the mechanisms inside is not reasonable damage.

Some teachers may find greater security by requiring parents to come to the school and check the pedometers out. However, this method will decrease the number of students who have access to a pedometer at home. The same permission slip can be used with this method.

Maintaining Pedometers

As with any mechanical device, pedometers require maintenance. Fortunately, the maintenance is minimal. It includes periodically checking the pedometers for accuracy and changing the batteries. These two tasks are quick and easy to perform. Older, more responsible students may be trained to assist with these tests.

Checking for Accuracy

One method of checking for accuracy is the "shake test." This test involves using the small plastic storage box seen in figure 3.3. These boxes can be purchased at most discount retail stores. The following is the procedure for conducting a shake test.

1. Reset all pedometers and place them vertically in the box. Two pedometers will fit in each "pocket."
2. Close the lid and use a rubber band to secure it.
3. Shake the box with a cadence similar to brisk walking.
4. Check the pedometers for accuracy. All pedometers should be within 5 percent of each other. For example, if most of the pedometers read 72 to 74 counts and one reads 65 counts, the low-reading pedometer may need new batteries or repair.
5. Repeat the test two or three times before making conclusions.

Another method of checking pedometers for accuracy is a "walk test." This test involves several people wearing the pedometers and walking a set number of steps. A "walk test" is performed as follows:

1. Fasten a pedometer to the waist.
2. Reset the pedometer.
3. Take 100 steps.
4. On the 100th step, stop and record the number of steps taken.

Again, the pedometer counts should not vary more than 5 percent. Perform the test twice for each pedometer.

Changing Batteries

Pedometers are powered by small, watch-type batteries. Generally, the battery placed in the pedometer by the manufacturer will last approximately 2 years. Unfortunately, most pedometers do not simply stop working when the battery is low, but rather their level of accuracy slowly decreases. An accuracy test every 1.5 to 2 years is necessary. Before changing batteries, perform an accuracy test and purchase batteries accordingly. To determine the type of battery needed and how to change it, consult the pedometer's manufacturer or distributor or the operating instructions that may have come with the pedometer. If the pedometer remains inaccurate after the battery is replaced, consult the distributor.

Selecting Pedometers

How many pedometers are needed? What type of pedometer is suitable? This section will provide the answers to these questions and will provide appropriate information necessary to make an educated selection of pedometers.

How Many Pedometers Should I Purchase?

When purchasing pedometers for physical education, class size is the critical factor. There should be one pedometer for each student in the class. Although the activities in this book can be adapted for classes with one pedometer for every two or three students, it is best that each student have a pedometer. Most likely, because of cost, one set of pedometers will be purchased and rotated among classes.

As with any piece of equipment, the long-term goal is to accumulate an adequate number of pedometers so that they can be used in many different situations, such as some students taking pedometers home. Therefore, the number of pedometers should exceed the number of students in the largest physical education class. We suggest that pedometer purchases be based on the largest class size plus 20 percent extra to cover loss, breakage, and theft. In other words, for a class of 30 students, purchase 36 pedometers.

What Type of Pedometer Should I Purchase?

There are numerous pedometers on the market, and as with any product, the quality varies depending on the manufacturer and cost. The Yamax pedometer, manufactured in Japan, has been used predominantly in research studies and is regarded as accurate and reliable (Welk et al. 2000). Other types of pedometers range from basic models that simply count steps to more complex models that measure steps, distance, activity time, and calories expended. For physical education purposes, a simple model that counts steps is more than adequate. Some of the newer pedometers appear to be as accurate as the Yamax models, and they may be attractive to students because they are available in different colors and have features such as delayed reset buttons and activity timers.

How Much Should I Pay for Pedometers?

Prices for pedometers range from $24 for one pedometer to as low as $12 each when large quantities are purchased. Bells and whistles may increase the price—from $20 pedometers on TV infomercials to $40 counters with compasses and clocks designed for hikers. Costs are increased by the addition of supplementary items such as teacher kits, special containers, and safety straps (to avoid dropping).

Identifying Funding Sources for Pedometers

For many schools, the money to purchase pedometers may not be in the physical education budget or even in the school's budget. Therefore, be creative, persistent, and patient when trying to obtain pedometers. The following sources, opportunities, and means of obtaining pedometers are available to most physical educators.

Local Businesses

Local businesses are often interested in supporting schools in their area. Donating to schools is not only good public relations but also a productive form of advertising. For physical education to benefit from the generosity of local businesses, three steps are necessary.

1. Contact the business owners with a phone call, letter, or, preferably, a face-to-face meeting.

2. Show the business owners the benefits of supplying pedometers to the school, in terms of both physical activity for the students and future business for the business owners. A short handout and discussion that explains how pedometers will be used to promote lifestyle activity, followed with how using pedometers benefits the school, community, and most important their business based on the initial chapters of this book, should provide a convincing presentation.

3. Invite the business owners to visit the school and participate in a physical education lesson that utilizes pedometers. Getting adults to participate in a lesson is an effective way to communicate the importance of a quality physical education program.

Again, persistence is critical. This effort may require meeting with numerous business owners and hearing "no" repeatedly. However, exposing business leaders to quality physical education will build bridges that pay off in the future.

Parent Organizations

Parent organizations are often a source of funding. As with businesses, receiving money from the parent organizations requires extensive "leg" work. A relationship can be developed with members of the organization by attending meetings, helping with fund-raisers, and giving positive feedback about their children. Another avenue for developing rapport with parents in the community is to hold Physical Education Nights. These nights can be staged with students demonstrating the program (e.g., Physical Education Demo Night) or with parents and students participating together (e.g., Family Night). Obviously, not all students in the school can meet on the same evening, but staggering these events for different grade levels throughout the year is a great way of developing public relations with parents.

I. Personal introduction
II. Shifting paradigm in physical education
    a. Fitness testing
        i. Use
        ii. Limitations
    b. Promoting lifestyle activity is the focus of physical education
    c. Need for physical activity
        i. Decrease all-cause mortality
        ii. Students' activity tracks
III. Measuring physical activity
    a. Brief discussion of all methods
    b. Pedometer most feasible
        i. Cost
        ii. Unobtrusive
        iii. Reliable and valid
IV. Uses of pedometers
    a. Teach students
    b. Improve teaching
    c. Improve the program
    (During this portion of the presentation, the specific benefits of pedometer use for the audience are included.)
V. Specific needs
    a. Number of pedometers and why
    b. Cost per pedometer and total cost
    c. Maintenance
VI. Questions
VII. Thank the audience for their time and consideration

Figure 3.4   Pedometer presentation outline.

Once a relationship is established and parents know about the physical education program at their children's school, the next step is to ask for a few minutes at a meeting to request funding for pedometers. Make a short presentation that explains the benefits of physical activity and how pedometers in physical education can help promote lifestyle activity. (See figure 3.4 for an example of a presentation outline.) During this presentation, stress to parents that pedometers are being requested to benefit their children now as well as in the future.

Universities

Because pedometers are an efficient way to measure physical activity, many universities are beginning to use them for research. One critical component of research is recruitment of people willing to participate in studies. Researchers may be interested in studying students, their parents, other adults (teachers, staff), or a combination of these populations. Contact local universities, specifically physical education departments (other departmental names include kinesiology, exercise science, exercise and wellness, and health), to see if they would like to conduct research in a school setting. Researchers are willing to compensate participants or those who recruit participants (e.g., physical education teachers) for studies. They have access to an abundance of pedometers through grants, university funds, and other sources. Thus, one method of compensating participants can be to donate pedometers.

Getting money from one organization, even if it is not enough for a full set of pedometers, is a good start. Combining donations from more than one source is acceptable and is often necessary. When attempting to secure funds for the purchase of pedometers, do not be discouraged by the word "no." There are many options. With determination and imagination, any teacher can generate the necessary funds to purchase pedometers and enhance his or her physical education program.

As is evident by the contents of this chapter, acquiring pedometers for your school requires initiative on your part. You must be a salesperson, a politician, and a motivational speaker as well as a teacher, and you must be relentless in pursuit of your goal. Once you've purchased your pedometers, your work is still not done. You must develop procedures that ensure efficient use of the pedometers as well as minimize loss, damage, and theft. These tasks may seem daunting, but taken in small steps, they are achievable, and your students will be the ultimate benefactors of your dedication to promoting lifestyle activity through quality physical education.

Increasing Visibility for Activity Promotion Programs

Good public relations can benefit physical educators in many ways. Making the public aware of a quality physical education program is a way to gain financial support. Showing parents how the physical education program promotes lifetime physical activity for their children can improve rapport with the community and reverse the negative image many people have of physical education.

Because parents influence the physical activity patterns of their children (Brustad 1993, 1996; Kimiecik and Horn 1998; Freedson and Evenson 1991), they are very important public relations targets when promoting lifestyle activity for students. Thus physical educators must not only educate students but also educate parents. Include them when designing lifestyle activity promotion programs.

There are numerous ways to contact parents and generate positive public sentiment. The most effective way is to send a letter explaining the physical education program, its rules, its purpose, and how students will be assessed. A follow-up letter can explain what pedometers are, why they are used, and how the students will use them in physical education. If students are allowed to take pedometers home (see page 29 for details), this policy should be mentioned in the letter.

Another method of developing good public relations is surprise calls at home. These calls are quick, positive reports on the behavior and accomplishments of students. A common objective is to contact 10 parents a week. Also, as discussed earlier in this chapter, conducting a pedometer activity night is an effective way to generate positive publicity for your program. Chapter 7 includes many ideas for using pedometers to promote lifestyle activity for the entire family.

Integrating Pedometer Activities Into the Classroom

Because of increased pressure for students to perform well on standardized tests, many physical education teachers are being asked to integrate academic subject matter into their curriculums. Cooperating with classroom teachers can create goodwill and positive feelings toward physical education. It also gives classroom teachers exposure to physical education that they may not have received otherwise. Using pedometers in the school setting provides many opportunities to integrate several academic subjects into physical education.

This effort requires working closely with classroom teachers and other teachers from the media, music, and art departments. It is helpful to accumulate as much specific information as possible on topics taught in the classroom. Physical education teachers and classroom teachers can then brainstorm and generate ideas on ways to integrate pedometer data with classroom topics. Many such ideas are presented in later chapters. They are marked with the integration icon (i.e., books). The following are brief examples of how to integrate pedometer data into other subject areas.

1. Teach the students about hypothesis testing in science by having them create hypotheses about their levels of activity in physical education classes. Have the students collect their step-count data, test their hypotheses, and write short reports about their experiments.

2. Have the students enter the same data in spreadsheets and generate graphs of their activity levels over several physical education

classes. Have the students complete the assignment by writing papers that interpret their graphs. This will integrate computers and English into the class.

3. Have the students use math, history, and geography skills to calculate the number of miles (kilometers) they walk in one month of physical education classes, and then have them route themselves to historically significant locations and write reports on the area.

Pedometer Writing Prompts for Classroom Teachers

Classroom teachers are continually searching for authentic writing prompts for students. The three types of writing—narrative, expository, and persuasive—can serve both the classroom teacher and the physical education teacher. Cross-curriculum integration can be implemented to demonstrate students' understanding of the importance of physical activity to long-term health and thus provide assessment for physical education teachers. At the same time, classroom teachers may draw on students' experiences in physical education classes to teach writing skills. The following prompts provide valid and relevant issues for students who have had experiences with pedometer use.

• Narrative writing tells about an event, describes feelings, and provides reactions. Have the students describe their days spent wearing pedometers and address such questions as "What did the pedometer tell you about yourself?" "How did you feel about what you learned?" "What types of things did you do during those days and what things do you think were best for your health?" "Are there things that you do that are not good for you?"

• Expository writing explains something or describes how something is done. Directions and reports are given objectively. Have the students write papers that explain what pedometers measure and why the information is important, why and how pedometers should be worn, or how to put them on and when to wear them.

• Persuasive writing takes a position and uses reasoning to persuade others to take the same position. Have the students write papers that try to persuade someone to wear a pedometer by explaining why it is important and what benefits it will provide.

Other Intervention Programs

Although physical education class is the most common place to develop physical activity intervention programs for students, other types of programs are used throughout the United States. For example, the state of Arizona uses a program called Promoting Lifestyle Activity for Youth

(P.L.A.Y.) (Pangrazi, 1999) in many of its schools. This program, sponsored by the Arizona Department of Health Services, incorporates activity breaks conducted by the classroom teacher into the school day. Pedometers are now being used in the program to promote student and family activity and to assess the effectiveness of the program. The book *Active Youth* (Samman 1998) provides numerous ideas for promoting lifestyle activities for students. A number of guidelines for developing a quality program are listed. Many exemplary programs that meet Centers for Disease Control and Prevention guidelines are also described in detail.

A new activity monitoring program has been added to the Fitnessgram program developed by the Cooper Institute (1999). This program is titled the Activitygram, and it includes a component for using pedometers to measure daily steps. The purposes of the Activitygram are to increase student awareness about their current activity levels and to offer incentives for increasing daily activity.

Regardless of where or by whom a program is implemented, pedometers are a useful method for assessing and promoting physical activity. Data collection with pedometers is simple, and the data are easy to interpret. Physical education intervention programs are fundamental to the effort to increase the activity levels of all students. However, to fully optimize these programs, teachers must constantly assess and modify them. This process is ongoing, lending itself to the use of feasible and valid assessment tools such as pedometers. By using data collected from the pedometer, teachers and other practitioners can strengthen their programs and promote lifestyle activity for all children.

If You Want to Know More . . .

These Web sites are a good place to search for the type of pedometers you want to purchase. Always contact the companies to see if a better price can be negotiated when pedometers are purchased in quantity.

Web Sites

www.walk4life.com

This Web site provides a catalog of pedometers, physical education teacher kits, pedometer tips, and accessories.

Books

To find other methods of organizing and managing elementary students see:

Darst, P.W. and R.P. Pangrazi. 2001. *Dynamic physical education for secondary school students (4th ed.)*. San Francisco: Benjamin Cummings.

Graham, G., S.A. Holt/Hale, and M. Parker. 2001. *Children moving: A reflective approach to teaching physical education (5th ed.).* Mountain View, CA: Mayfield.

Pangrazi, R.P. 2001. *Dynamic physical education for elementary school students (13th ed).* Boston: Allyn and Bacon.

References

Brustad, R.J. 1993. Who will go out and play? Parental and psychological influences on children's attraction to physical activity. *Pediatr. Exerc. Sci.* 5:210–23.

—1996. Attraction to physical activity in urban schoolchildren: Parental socialization and gender influences. *Res. Q. Exercise Sport* 67:316–23.

Cooper Institute. 1999. *Fitnessgram test administration manual (2nd ed.).* Champaign, IL: Human Kinetics.

Freedson, P.S. and S. Evenson. 1991. Familial aggregation in physical activity. *Res. Q. Exercise Sport* 62:384–89.

Kimiecik, J.C. and T.S. Horn. 1998. Parental beliefs and children's moderate-to-vigorous physical activity. *Res. Q. Exercise Sport* 69:163–75.

Pangrazi, R.P. 1999. *Promoting lifetime activity for youth.* Phoenix: Arizona Department of Health Services.

Samman, P. 1998. *Active youth: Ideas for implementing CDC physical activity promotion guidelines.* Champaign, IL: Human Kinetics.

Welk, G.J., F.A. Differding, R.W. Thompson, S.N. Blair, J. Dziura, and P. Hart. 2000. The utility of the Digi-Walker step counter to assess daily physical activity patterns. *Med. Sci. Sport Exer.* 32:S481–88.

Basic Pedometer Activities

During a staff meeting, the principal of Woodlake Elementary School announced a new "growth" project for the faculty. Members of each department were to develop a new method for improving their department's program. The method was to focus on assessment and using that information to make improvements. The improvements could pertain to the entire program, the curriculum, the teaching, or even a single objective; however, the method was expected to be innovative and not require extensive work by the faculty. The principal explained that many techniques are overused and she wanted the faculty to be creative. After the meeting, members of the physical education department met to begin planning. Although they were not sure what aspect of their program to assess, they knew they wanted to use the pedometers they had worked diligently to acquire through business donations.

This chapter will present a variety of methods for using pedometers to improve physical activity intervention programs. Although the emphasis here is on physical education, physical activity intervention programs are not limited to physical education settings. Because of the strong interest in physical activity promotion in the United States, many school-based physical activity intervention programs have emerged. Some programs are offered by communities, and others are sponsored at the state and national levels. For example, the President's Council on Physical Activity and Fitness has developed an activity promotion program that offers students a chance to earn the Presidential Active Lifestyle Award (President's Council on Physical Fitness and Sports 2002). Obviously, because most children are exposed to physical education, this setting provides much potential for effective intervention.

Regardless of the setting, pedometers can enhance the effectiveness of an activity intervention program by providing valuable feedback for a program assessment. Other uses of pedometers are discussed in later chapters. Also, many programs outside the school setting use physical education teachers to contact participants. Therefore, physical education teachers most often are central figures in physical activity intervention programs for students. The purpose of this chapter is to illustrate how pedometer step-count data can be used for many different purposes, all of which can increase the effectiveness of physical activity programs.

Lifestyle physical activity is now the focus of quality physical education programs. Thus, an overriding objective of physical education is to increase the activity level of students. Quality physical education teachers consistently generate new ideas as they attempt to improve their programs. These ideas may include altering teaching techniques or developing new teaching skills. Also, these teachers reflect on their lessons and curriculum to discern changes that can increase the effectiveness of their programs. Pedometers can help teachers to quantify physical activity as they seek the best activity intervention programs for their students.

Pedometers and Accountability

One question heard by teachers in all areas is "What evidence is there that you're teaching your students anything?" Using a current buzzword, the question becomes "How do you demonstrate accountability?" With the changing fitness/activity paradigm and the emergence of pedometers, this question can now be answered with objective data. Collecting the step counts of students and measuring their physical activity levels provides the necessary data. These data allow physical education teachers to make productive changes in existing curricula or teaching practices.

The question "How do I know if my students are active enough?" is a pertinent one. The physical activity guidelines presented in chapter 1 recommending 60 minutes of daily activity can serve as the foundation for physical activity (see page 7). Other research indicates that in a 30-minute physical education lesson using developmentally appropriate activities, students averaged slightly less than 1,500 steps (Beighle and Pangrazi 2000). This study assessed students in second through sixth grades and found the step count to be relatively similar across grades. Teachers in this study were asked not to alter their instructions to promote step counts, such as telling students to walk in place or move while directions were being given. The findings from this study provide teachers with a ballpark estimate of how active students should be during physical education classes. Although students may not be moving throughout the entire lesson, the time in which students are active provides a significant head start on the 30 to 60 minutes of recommended daily activity.

Consider other variables that may influence the activity levels of students. Step counts may vary depending on the time of year, region of the country, or other factors. However, these factors should not be used as an excuse for low activity levels. Regardless of environmental influences, students everywhere should accumulate adequate physical activity on a daily basis.

Recent research has examined the average number of steps accumulated each day for children all over the world. A study by Vincent and Pangrazi (2001) involving over 700 boys and girls 6 to 12 years of age showed that the average number of steps taken by children did not decrease between the ages of 6 and 12 years. The study revealed that boys averaged 13,000 steps over a 24-hour period, and girls averaged approximately 11,000 steps. This study refutes past beliefs that children become much less active as they age (Rowland 1990). However, it does appear that as children enter adolescence, their physical activity levels decline, necessitating the promotion of physical activity for students in this age group.

Pedometer Activities in the Physical Education Program

How active are your students? Are some students more active than others? Do your lessons give students ample opportunity for activity? Both you and your students need to know the answers to these questions. Certainly, there are other goals in physical education classes, but physical activity has a high priority. An important instructional issue is designing a lesson that finds the "sweet spot" in the physical activity continuum. For example, when an instructor "rolls out the ball," there will likely be quite a bit of physical activity, especially for the gifted students. However, opportunities for less gifted students may be limited. The flip side is a lesson in which little equipment is used and students must take turns. The result is little activity and little learning. Quality lessons are usually characterized by efficient instruction and maximum activity. Pedometers can be used to determine whether there is adequate activity. Following are lessons that form the basis for conducting many of the pedometer activities in this book. Regardless of the age of the student, these basic activities must be learned before those in later chapters are attempted. These learning modules will not only help students learn about physical activity but also offer some insight into the amount of activity students receive in class.

▶ Establish a Daily Student Step-Count Baseline

Many factors influence the daily activity levels of students (e.g., lesson content, weather). Thus, it is best to collect data over several days to establish a meaningful activity baseline. The most common method of establishing a baseline is to collect 4 days of data for elementary school students and 8 days of data for secondary school students. More collection days are recommended for older students because their activity patterns are more variable than those of elementary school students. See form 4.1 for a worksheet on establishing baseline activity levels for students.

Purpose

1. To learn how many steps are taken on a daily basis
2. To calculate and understand the method for establishing a daily baseline step-count level
3. To understand how to set a personal goal once the baseline step count has been determined

Activity Description

1. Have the students check out pedometers between 8:00 and 8:30 A.M. with baseline step-count and goal forms (see form 4.1).
2. The next day in the classroom, between 8:00 and 8:30 A.M., let the students record their baseline step counts for day 1 on the form. Continue this procedure for 4 days for elementary school students and 8 days for middle and secondary school students.
3. After the requisite number of days of step counts has been gathered, compute the baseline daily step count.
4. Calculate the step-count goal based on the baseline daily step count (see form 4.1)
5. After a class has gathered data for the requisite number of days, the pedometers are rotated to another class and the process is repeated.

Setting Personal Activity Goals
With Pedometers

Your goal should be based on how active you are most days. Do not compare your performance with others because everyone has different capabilities.

The first thing you have to do is find your baseline activity level.

Calculate Your Baseline Step Counts

Elementary school students	Middle/high school students
Day 1 step counts _____ Day 2 step counts _____ Day 3 step counts _____ Day 4 step counts _____ Total step counts _____ divided by 4 equals _____. This number is your **baseline activity** and will be used to determine your personal activity goal.	Day 1 step counts _____ Day 2 step counts _____ Day 3 step counts _____ Day 4 step counts _____ Day 5 step counts _____ Day 6 step counts _____ Day 7 step counts _____ Day 8 step counts _____ Total step counts _____ divided by 8 equals _____. This number is your **baseline activity** and will be used to determine your personal activity goal.

Next, calculate your personal step-count goal as shown in the examples.

Calculate Your Step-Count Goal

Baseline	Personal goal (10% of your baseline plus your baseline)	Weeks	Total step counts
4,000 steps	4,000 x .10 = 400 steps + 4,000	1 and 2	4,400
	Every 2 weeks thereafter, the goal will be increased by 400 steps.	3 and 4	4,800
		5 and 6	5,200
		7 and 8	5,600
		9 and 10	6,000
6,000 steps	6,000 x .10 = 600 steps + 6,000	1 and 2	6,600
	Every 2 weeks thereafter, the goal will be increased by 600 steps.	3 and 4	7,200
		5 and 6	7,800
		7 and 8	8,400
		9 and 10	9,000

From *Pedometer Power: 67 Lessons for K–12* by Robert P. Pangrazi, Aaron Beighle, and Cara L. Sidman, 2003, Champaign, IL: Human Kinetics.

▶Establish a Step-Count Baseline for Physical Education Lessons

How many steps should students take during a 30-minute lesson? Usually, the range varies from 1,200 to 2,000 steps. Keating (2001) estimates the number to be closer to 1,200 steps.

Purpose

1. To learn how many steps your students take
2. To establish a class average for steps

Activity Description

To identify the current baseline for steps in your class, do the following:

1. Arrange the pedometers on the stage or around the perimeter of the teaching area with forms that have the students' names and blank spaces for recording the data (see form 4.2). Alternatively, organize the students into squads and then group the pedometers accordingly. Students quickly learn the routine of attaching pedometers to their belts.

2. When all the students have their pedometers properly secured, ask them to stand still and reset their pedometers so that everybody starts with zero step counts.

3. Make sure the pedometers are kept closed during the entire lesson. Before the end of the class period, have the students take their pedometers back to where the pedometers were picked up and record their step counts on the form.

4. Conduct a minimum of four lessons for all the students to get an accurate representation of how much activity has been accumulated. Variation exists among different types of lessons. Measuring four different lessons and finding an average score better indicates the activity levels in your classes.

5. From the data gathered, compute the class average and let the class know the average number of steps taken. If desired, it might be helpful to suggest ways to become more active to the entire class.

▶Increase Activity Levels Within Physical Education Classes

An important strategy for improving instructional effectiveness is to use the baseline step-count data to set teaching goals. Lessons vary in terms of physical activity level. For example, a jogging or walking lesson would

Student Activity Baseline
for Physical Education Lessons

Name _____   Class _____   Pedometer # _____

Content of lesson	Number of steps in class	Date
Day 1:		
Day 2:		
Day 3:		
Day 4:		
Day 5:		
Day 6:		
Day 7:		
Day 8:		

From *Pedometer Power: 67 Lessons for K–12* by Robert P. Pangrazi, Aaron Beighle, and Cara L. Sidman, 2003, Champaign, IL: Human Kinetics.

undoubtedly result in a higher number of accumulated steps than a juggling lesson. Despite this wide variation, maximizing the amount of steps taken in physical education class is a reasonable goal. One way is to alternate low-activity and high-activity instruction. Some of our data have shown that the majority of students accumulate only 4,000 steps during the school day. If 2,000 of those steps are gathered in a 30-minute physical education lesson, it is critical that activity be maximized in the sedentary school environment.

Purpose

1. To identify the activity level of physical education lessons with differing content
2. To learn to alternate low-intensity and high-intensity activities

Activity Description

1. Assuming you have more than one class at each grade level, use this situation to determine how effectively you can modify the physical

education environment to ensure adequate activity for your students. Teach one class without any modification to the lesson.

2. Change how you teach the second class. Identify an intervention (treatment) that you can implement to increase the amount of activity in your lesson. Here are some suggestions:
   - Add an active game.
   - Ask the students to walk around the area while they practice their skills.
   - Let the students practice with a partner, on the condition that they must be moving.
   - Add a high-intensity activity such as rope jumping.

3. Gather data on both classes and compare the activity levels. Form 4.3 is a data form on which to record and average student activity data. Reflect on the lessons. Did adding more activity increase or reduce the effectiveness of your instruction? Did the students seem more enthusiastic or less enthusiastic about learning? Determine how this action research can be used in future lessons based on your reflections. The point again is to help the students accumulate

Form 4.3

Increasing Activity Levels in Physical Education Classes

Teacher _____   Lesson content: _____   Date _____

Student	Number of steps each day				
	Mon.	Tues.	Wed.	Thurs.	Fri.
Average per day					

as much activity as possible. The school environment is primarily a sedentary experience, making an active physical education lesson very important.

▶Increase Physical Activity During Discretionary Time

Even though the school day is heavily structured, with most time spent in a sedentary setting, students have some discretionary time. The most obvious discretionary times occur before school, during recess, during lunch hour, and after school. In the morning, students stand outside the school door waiting for it to open. Even though recess looks like an active setting, most students are sitting or standing still. These discretionary times are unique opportunities to increase the overall activity levels of students, and pedometers can show students how easy it is to increase their physical activity during their free time.

Purpose

1. To teach students about their activity levels during free time
2. To increase the amount of step counts students accumulate during their discretionary time

Activity Description

1. Choose one class to wear the pedometers for the week (assuming only one set of pedometers is available for an entire class).
2. Prepare the pedometers and record forms (see form 4.4) for use in the homeroom class the first thing each morning. Have the students put on the pedometers on arrival at school and wear them throughout the day. Say nothing to students except that the pedometers will gather activity data and all they have to do is wear them. Gather 2 days of data without discussion. The homeroom teacher collects the pedometers at the end of the day, and the students record their number of steps on their record cards.
3. At the end of the second day of data gathering, discuss the baseline data with the students. Introduce your desired intervention plan to the class. Ask each student to try to increase the number of accumulated steps by 10 percent over the next 2 days. Encourage students to select activities they enjoy from among the following intervention strategies:
   - Don't sit or stand still during recess and lunch-hour times.
   - Get involved in a game.

Form 4.4

Increasing Physical Activity During Discretionary Time

Name _____ Class _____ Pedometer # _____

Activity	Steps accumulated	Date
Pre-intervention steps accumulated		
Day 1		
Day 2		
Post-intervention steps accumulated		
Day 3		
Day 4		

From *Pedometer Power: 67 Lessons for K–12* by Robert P. Pangrazi, Aaron Beighle, and Cara L. Sidman, 2003, Champaign, IL: Human Kinetics.

- Walk and talk with a friend.
- Practice a physical skill such as rope jumping, shooting baskets, or dribbling a soccer ball.
- Play hopscotch or Frisbee golf.

4. Record the step counts for each day of intervention. Chart the data and compare the first 2 days of activity with the second 2 days. Discuss how many more steps students accumulated by making active choices and performing things they like to do.

5. Give the pedometers to a new class and repeat the entire process.

▶ Calculate Stride Length   MATH

There are times when you want to know how far you have walked rather than how many steps you have taken. You may want to calculate how many miles you walked in one day so that you can estimate how far you have hiked or jogged. There are a number of ways to measure your stride length (the distance you cover with one step), and two of the best ways are described next.

Purpose

To measure stride length

Activity Description

1. *The 100-foot (30.5-meter) walk.* Measure a distance of 100 feet and mark the start and finish lines. Walk at a normal pace from one line to the other and count the number of steps you take. To calculate stride length, divide 100 by the number of steps you have taken. For example, if you take 40 steps to cover the 100 feet, your stride length will be 100 feet divided by 40, which equals 2.5 feet (.76 meter) per stride.

2. *Wet foot walk.* Another way to measure stride length is to walk through a water puddle onto dry pavement and measure the heel-to-heel distance of the wet footprints. Be certain to measure from heel to heel or from toe to toe, not from the heel of one footprint to the toe of another.

Convert Steps to Mileage   MATH

Many students want to know how far they walk, but step counts don't give that information. Once students know how far they walk, they can easily convert steps to miles and calculate how long it will take to walk certain routes or hike trails.

Purpose

To calculate total distance covered in feet, yards, and miles (meters and kilometers)

Activity Description

1. Have the students determine the length of their stride (in feet or meters) as discussed in the earlier section.

2. Have the students multiply their number of accumulated steps by their stride lengths. For example, a student who has walked 1,200 steps multiplies that number by his or her stride length. Assume the stride length is 2.75 feet (.84 meter) multiplied by 1,200 steps. The distance walked is 3,300 feet (1,006 meters).

3. Convert feet to mileage by dividing 5,280 (the number of feet in a mile) into the number of feet walked (convert meters to kilometers by dividing 1,000 into the number of meters walked). In this example, 3,300 divided by 5,280 equals .625 mile (1,006 divided by 1,000 equals 1.006 kilometers).

Set Individual Activity Goals   COMPUTERS

Pedometers are excellent tools for teaching students to set activity goals. When students learn to monitor their daily activity and to set goals, they begin to accept responsibility for accumulating adequate daily activity. Achieving goals is not a competitive endeavor; it is a personal matter for each student. The focus of activity goals is to make students aware of how active they are and how active they need to be for good health. With this knowledge, they can modify their daily activity if it falls below the good-health threshold based on pedometer data rather than on a guess.

Purpose

1. To teach students how to set personal activity goals based on pedometer step counts
2. To teach students to log daily physical activity
3. To teach students to chart their physical activity data in a spreadsheet

Activity Description

1. Design a personal goal form (see form 4.5) that allows the students to log their activities, record how many steps they have taken, and set personal goals.
2. Have the students secure a pedometer as described in "Introducing Pedometers to Students" in chapter 3 on page 22. The students can clear their pedometers and start their step counts as soon as they are ready.
3. Gather 3 to 4 weeks of physical education class activity data so that the students can see whether they are achieving their personal goals.
4. If possible, allow the students to go to the computer lab and chart their data in an electronic spreadsheet. Review the data by asking questions such as
   - Did your step counts change because of different types of activities?
   - What is a reasonable goal?
   - How many steps should you try to increase each week (5 to 10 percent)?
   - How can you accumulate more steps in physical education class and during free time?

Variations

1. With cooperation of the classroom teachers, this process can be done with the students wearing the pedometers during the entire school day and recording step counts.
2. If feasible, send the pedometers home over the weekend and ask students to share their data with their parents.

My Personal Goal Card

Initials _____   Pedometer Number _____   Teacher _____

Week 1

Date	Activity	Steps

My goal for week 2 is:

Week 2

Date	Activity	Steps

My goal for week 3 is:

Week 3

Date	Activity	Steps

From *Pedometer Power: 67 Lessons for K–12* by Robert P. Pangrazi, Aaron Beighle, and Cara L. Sidman. 2003, Champaign, IL: Human Kinetics.

▶Create Cooperative Class Goals

Goal setting can also be used as a class project. The process is very similar to setting individual goals, except that the whole class decides on a common goal. This common goal setting helps students learn to establish cooperative goals in which everyone must succeed for the group to succeed.

Purpose

1. To teach students to set group goals
2. To teach students to cooperate with the entire class
3. To teach students to encourage others in the class
4. To teach students to think about ways to increase physical activity

Activity Description

1. Have the students record on form 4.5 their physical education step counts each day for 1 week.
2. At the end of the week, total the number of steps accumulated by the class during physical education.
3. On the first day of physical education class the following week, tell the class their total step count. Then discuss a goal for the coming week.
4. Each time the class total is given, discuss a new goal.

Variations

1. Perform this activity with small groups of students during physical education.
2. Set goals for 15-minute increments during one physical education lesson.
3. Have the students wear the pedometers during school for the entire week. The class can estimate or guess how many steps they will accumulate during school. This exercise will foster discussions on how to increase daily physical activity levels.
4. Have the students convert step counts into miles or kilometers and relate them to a similar distance in the area (e.g., from Main Street to the elementary school).

Teaching Hints

1. Never disclose student data without the student's permission. Similarly, never force students to reveal their step counts, neither to a teacher, to another student, nor on a form.

2. If only pedometer numbers are used to identify students, designate students to total the accumulated steps. Avoid asking students to calculate the other students' data. Inevitably someone will find out their classmates' data and compromise privacy.

3. If the class does not achieve its goal, discuss why not. Explain that some physical education lessons may be more active than others (e.g., rhythmic activities versus softball).

4. Encourage all students to be positive about the class goal and supportive of each other. Do not tolerate negative comments about step counts.

Improve Instruction Using Pedometer Data

What if the data are collected and analyzed, and they reveal that the students are inactive? Does it mean the program is ineffective? No. Does it mean improvements can be made? Yes, all programs can improve. Even if the data revealed the students to be adequately active, other ways to further increase their physical activity levels can be found. The following are some areas to analyze if increased physical activity is a goal for physical education classes.

Instructional Time

How long are your instructions? Many teachers have a tendency to give lengthy instructions, thus decreasing the amount of activity time. Certainly, it does not make sense to eliminate instruction to increase physical activity time. A better solution is to break up the instruction into 15- to 30-second episodes followed by 60 to 90 seconds of activity or practice time. This approach is much more efficient for young students, who are usually able to concentrate on only one or two points at a time.

Management Time

Managing and moving students into formations takes time. Often, it is done with students standing around or counting off, not only inviting discipline problems but also creating a time of inactivity and boredom. Some ways to group students include getting them into a circle, having them find partners, or getting them equipped while keeping them moving and behaving responsibly. Minimizing management time and teaching management skills on the move will increase the amount of activity time and raise the enjoyment level of the lesson (Darst and Pangrazi 2002; Pangrazi 2001).

Selection and Modification of Activities

Some types of lessons lend themselves to inactivity. For example, relay races tend to have lower levels of activity because students must wait for a turn to run. Also, if lessons are organized so that students must wait in line and take turns, the amount of activity time will be reduced. Regularly examining instructional activities to ensure they offer everyone in the class the maximum amount of participation time will increase the likelihood of students being active and enjoying the experience. See chapter 5 for modifying lessons to increase activity.

Role Modeling

The way you act and move during physical education classes are important components of effective instruction. Teachers who stand in one place and do not move are likely to have classes that are similarly inactive. To promote activity among the students, move about the teaching area with vigor and enthusiasm. As the saying goes, "Enthusiasm and moving are contagious . . . spread them."

Lesson Type

Certain lessons in physical education provide less activity than others. It is your responsibility to increase activity in low-activity lessons. For instance, some schools require physical education teachers to include health instruction in their lessons. Rather than present a static health lesson, use activity as the medium to teach health concepts. Many physical education lessons are much more effective when students can learn on the move.

Environment

Does the environment encourage students to be active? If students are expected to be active and participate in a variety of activities, the physical education environment must be safe and nonthreatening. Students should have opportunities to discover ways to increase the activity in their physical education classes. A simple challenge such as, "Let's see how many different ways you can move while tossing your beanbags," can prompt students to increase their activity levels. Then different students can lead the class in performing their activity ideas.

If You Want to Know More . . .

Fortunately, there is much information for teachers related to increasing physical activity and enhancing physical fitness. The Web sites that follow offer both practical and research information that is written for teachers. The references offer in-depth information about how to use pedometers and how accurately they measure steps.

Web Sites

www.aahperd.org
American Alliance for Health, Physical Education, Recreation and Dance

www.aahperd.org/naspe/template.cfm
National Association for Sport and Physical Education

www.indiana.edu/~preschal
The President's Challenge: Physical Activity and Fitness Awards Program

http://pe.central.vt.edu/index.html
PE Central is the premier Web site for health and physical education teachers.

www.americanfitness.net
This site from Human Kinetics offers information for teachers regarding the Fitnessgram, Activitygram, and Physical Best.

www.fitness.gov
The President's Council on Physical Fitness and Sports Web site offers current information and copies of the *Research Digest.*

www.pelinks4u.org
A good site for finding up-to-date techniques and information about teaching.

References

Beighle, A. and R.P. Pangrazi. 2000. The validity of six pedometers for measuring the physical activity of children. Unpublished manuscript.

Darst, P.W. and R.P. Pangrazi. 2002. *Dynamic physical education for secondary school students (4th ed.).* San Francisco: Benjamin Cummings.

Keating, T. 2001. *The power of the pedometer in physical education.* Chicago: Walk4Life, Inc.

Pangrazi, R.P. 2001. *Dynamic physical education for elementary school children (13th ed.).* Boston: Allyn and Bacon.

President's Council on Physical Fitness and Sports. 2002. The President's Challenge Physical Activity and Fitness Awards Program. Bloomington, IN: The President's Challenge.

Rowland, T.W. 1990. *Exercise and children's health.* Champaign, IL: Human Kinetics.

Vincent, S.V. and R.P. Pangrazi. 2001. *Determining baseline activity levels in children.* Unpublished doctoral dissertation, Arizona State University, Tempe.

Pedometer Activities for Elementary School Students

During the summer, Mr. Youngblood attended a workshop titled "Physical Fitness to Physical Activity: A Changing Paradigm." Although he was a veteran elementary physical education teacher with 12 years of experience, Mr. Youngblood was open to the new ideas presented at the workshop, particularly the use of pedometers in physical education. Using information he had gotten from the workshop, he was able to put together a presentation that convinced the parent association at his school to donate money to purchase one set of pedometers. Mr. Youngblood started using the pedometers immediately to record the step counts of the students in each of his classes. After accumulating data for several months, the students became bored and wanted to know what else they could do with the pedometers. Unfortunately, the workshop had only covered why pedometers should be used in physical education classes, not ways to use them. Now what?

Ideas in this chapter are useful for teachers like Mr. Youngblood, teachers on the cutting edge who are looking for ways to enhance their programs and promote lifestyle activity for their students. This chapter is filled with practical ideas that can help students understand their personal activity lifestyles. It will also help students choose activities that suit their activity needs.

Elementary Physical Education Pedometer Activities

The following activities assume a basic understanding of pedometer use. The activities in chapter 4 teach students how to use pedometers, establish baseline activity levels, set goals, and modify daily activity levels.

▶*Moving Across America*   SOCIAL STUDIES, MATH, ENGLISH

Once wearing pedometers and recording step counts have become routine, one way to show students how much activity they are accumulating during physical education is to implement Moving Across America. This activity allows students to add their total steps and then calculate the total number of miles walked using the procedure described in chapter 4 on page 51. Students can then track their own progress across a smaller designated area (city, county, or state) while the teacher tracks the class' progress across the United States. This activity is also an opportunity for teachers to integrate physical education with classroom subjects.

Purpose

1. To teach students the importance of physical activity
2. To allow students to record their total steps taken during physical education
3. To integrate physical activity into academic subjects, including social studies, math, and English

Activity Description

1. Explain to the class that they will track their progress across the designated area, and you will track the class' progress across the United States.
2. Give the students a map of a smaller area (city or county) on which to track their progress. A mileage scale should be shown on the

map. Predrawn routes with the corresponding distances labeled on the map may be useful (e.g., routes from cities to landmarks or from city to city).

3. Allow the students to wear pedometers and record their step counts in physical education class.

4. Total the number of steps the class has taken during physical education class.

5. Calculate the number of miles walked using each student's stride length (see chapter 4, page 51).

6. Allow the students to track their progress on their maps using predetermined routes or routes of their choosing.

7. Calculate and chart the total miles for each class on a large map of the United States.

Classroom Integration

Moving Across America can easily be integrated into classroom lessons. Classroom teachers can calculate step/mile (or step/kilometer) distances and map them during class time. The following are some suggestions for integrating this activity into classroom lessons.

1. As classes progress to different regions or states, the classroom teacher asks the students to find some unique geographic characteristics of the state or region. To learn directions, students determine what is north, south, east, or west of their current location.

2. An imaginary trip around the country can continue throughout the entire school year. Establish a route using the classroom teacher's yearly plan for history. As the students progress to different areas, the history of that area becomes a part of a history lesson. You briefly discuss physical activities common in that area or ask questions pertaining to the history lesson at the conclusion of class.

3. Teach developmentally appropriate rhythm routines using music from different regions or states. During a rhythm lesson, have the students identify the location the class has reached and use music from that region. For example, if the class is in Louisiana, use Cajun music.

4. Art class activities can be coordinated with pedometer use. Have the students make posters or other projects that advocate physical activity or a healthy lifestyle in the region they are currently "visiting" and use the posters to decorate the gymnasium or school.

5. Computers can be used to assist in all areas of Move Across America. Let the students use computers to track their progress, calculate

their total number of steps and convert that number to miles, research the geography or history of their current location, and make promotional posters advocating activity lifestyles.

▶ *Guess and Check*

One method of teaching students about physical activity and promoting lifestyle activity is by showing them the difference between active and inactive. Guess and Check is an activity that minimizes interruptions to the existing lesson. It encourages students to estimate the amount and type of physical activity they participate in on a daily basis.

Purpose

1. To teach students the difference between "active" and "inactive"
2. To teach students how to estimate step counts and distance
3. To allow students to estimate their own activity by measuring step counts and then checking their estimations

Activity Description

1. Have the students wear pedometers during several physical education lessons while making periodic checks of their step counts. They will become aware of how many steps they take during physical education class.
2. Introduce a variety of lessons that will produce a wide range of step counts. For example, a gymnastics lesson may produce fewer steps than a basketball lesson.
3. Explain to the class that they will be guessing and checking. Tell them what the lesson focus is and ask them to guess how many steps they will take during half of the class.
4. Halfway through the lesson, have the students check their step counts to see how close their guesses were. Ask them to reset the pedometers and make another guess based on your description of the activities for the remainder of class.
5. At the end of class, have the students check their pedometers again to see how close they were.
6. At the conclusion of class, ask the students why they think their guesses were incorrect or correct. Emphasize that an incorrect guess is okay because students will get better with practice and start to understand which activities are the most productive.
7. Repeat the procedure with a variety of lessons. Each time, when discussing the guesses, tie in previous lessons. Prompt the class

with questions such as, "Was gymnastics more active than basketball? Why or why not?"

Variations

1. A progression of this activity is to predict the number of steps taken for an entire lesson, based on the specific lesson type.
2. If a fitness component is incorporated into the lesson, the students can guess and check during the fitness portion as well. A discussion of the limitations of pedometers is necessary (i.e., pedometers only measure locomotor movement and not stationary activities such as strength exercises or stretches). Ask the question, "If a pedometer can't measure it, does that mean it's not good activity?"

▶Design a Route
GEOGRAPHY, MATH, ENGLISH

Several programs can be coordinated with pedometer step counts. For example, the Centers for Disease Control advocates a Walk to School program for students (see Web site **www.cdc.gov/nccdphp/dnpa/ kidswalk**). Teaching students how to choose safe routes with less traffic and fewer busy streets to cross is an important outcome of this activity.

Purpose

1. To provide students with the opportunity to design walking/jogging routes on and off school grounds
2. To add variety to a walking/jogging lesson
3. To encourage students to cooperate with classmates

Activity Description

1. Draw maps of the school area and the surrounding neighborhood and mark locations that are off-limits.
2. At the beginning of the lesson, discuss the importance of walking/ jogging in promoting health and fitness. Explain the importance of pace and walking with a friend. Discuss safety issues such as avoiding high-traffic streets, not talking to strangers, and walking where other students and parents walk.
3. Organize the students into groups of three or four. Ask each student to wear a pedometer.
4. Give each group a map of the school grounds. After they learn the school area, give them maps of the neighborhood.

5. Record the number of steps the students needed to walk their selected routes. Calculate the total score by adding the scores of all students in the group. Mark the legend for the map in steps.

Variations

1. Allow groups to switch maps and walk other routes.

2. Ask the students to guess how many steps the route will require before they start the walk.

3. Let the students use routes from other classes and see if their group has the same number of steps. Discuss why or why not?

Classroom Integration

Using the playground map, ask the students to spell their name or spelling-lesson words, make shapes, or draw pictures with their steps. Also, reinforce terms from academic areas, such as "perimeter" and "diagonal."

Graphing Step Counts

COMPUTERS, MATH, ENGLISH, SCIENCE

Once step counts have been collected for a few days or more, teach the students to chart and graph their step counts. The graphs give the students a visual representation of their physical activity. Graphing step counts is an opportunity for you to work with the computer or math teacher in the school. The students can record their step counts and then enter the data on simple electronic spreadsheets and graph the data in a variety of ways.

Purpose

1. To provide students with the opportunity to use a pedometer to measure activity

2. To produce a graphic representation of students' step counts for a given amount of time

3. To integrate physical activity and physical education into academic areas

Activity Description

1. Produce a graphic representation of the students' step counts for a given amount of time (see figure 5.1).

2. Ask the students to identify ways they can increase their physical activity. List their top five suggestions and test them to see if they are effective.

3. Ask the students to analyze the graph and write a brief discussion pertaining to their activity level. For example, a student might discuss why he or she was very active one day and relatively inactive the next.

Classroom Integration

1. Intermediate-grade students can also use step-count data and graphs to calculate means and predict future activity levels. The students can brainstorm to determine why they reached different levels of activity. Ask them to write short essays about their physical activity level according to the graph.
2. Guessing and making predictions based on the graph is an introduction to the scientific method. Have the students develop questions and hypotheses related to physical activity and step counts.

▶Develop a Personal Fitness Routine

Often, fitness regimens in physical education mandate that all students perform the same amount of physical activity. It is well established that wide variation exists among students and their ability to perform physical fitness activities (Pangrazi 2001). One way to personalize fitness routines in physical education is to give students pedometers to measure how many steps they take during their fitness routines.

Purpose

1. To monitor the level of fitness activity for each student
2. To offer students a chance to control the number of steps they accumulate during fitness activities

Activity Description

1. Design a fitness routine that alternates aerobic exercises with strength and flexibility exercises.
2. Ask the students to find a workout partner and give each team the following challenge: Accumulate a total of 1,200 steps. While one person does a strength or flexibility exercise, the other person does aerobic walking, running in place, or any other form of aerobic exercise for 30 to 60 seconds.
3. Have the students switch exercise roles after 30 to 60 seconds and continue until the 1,200 steps are accumulated.

The goal is to teach students to work together while learning that fitness is personal. In some pairs, one partner may accumulate 700 steps, whereas

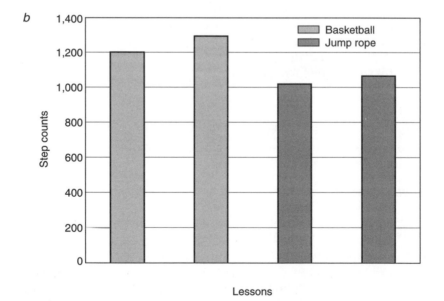

Figure 5.1 Charting and graphing pedometer data. *(a)* Drew's pedometer data chart and *(b)* Drew's pedometer data graph.

the other accumulates 500 steps. Teach them to record the steps performed during each interval and to total the number of accumulated steps.

▶Pedometer Orienteering
GEOGRAPHY, MATH

Orienteering is growing in popularity throughout the world. It combines hiking/walking with using a compass to find directions. Adding pedometers to orienteering can help students learn to estimate various distances and the number of steps required to cover those distances.

Purpose

1. To expose students to the lifestyle activity of orienteering
2. To teach students to find geographic coordinates using a compass
3. To teach students to estimate distances and read compass directions

Activity Description

1. Design an orienteering course in which different landmarks are used for visual sightings. Allow the students to work in small groups. Create enough markers for each group, depending on the size of the class. This arrangement allows each group to start at a different marker. Each marker should have directions, including visual sighting direction and distance to the next marker.
2. Once the sighting is made, the students walk a number of steps (give a range of steps because of different stride lengths) in that direction to a hoop. The students then refer to their direction sheet, which gives them a new visual sighting landmark and number of steps to travel. The goal is to reach all the hoops.
3. As the students navigate the course, move around the course and offer them feedback and support.

Figure 5.2 is a sample course that might be created using the school and playground area. Students can start anywhere on the course.

You can make this activity more difficult by putting directions to the next station at each checkpoint. This way, if the students don't find the stations, they will not be able to complete the course. Also, instead of visual sighting, the students can be directed by compass bearings and steps (for example, "from the monkey bars, take a compass bearing of 200 degrees and walk 325 steps"). Figure 5.3 shows sample directions for a beginning course and an intermediate course that incorporate bearings. See page 73 for more information about the use of the letters in figure 5.3.

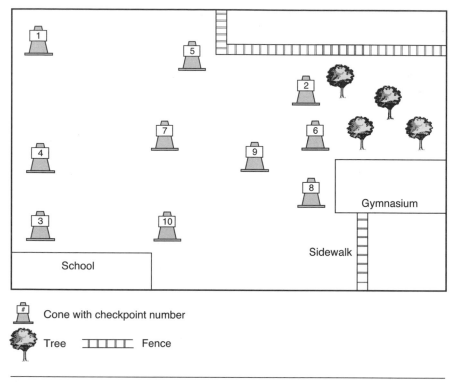

Figure 5.2   Sample orienteering course.

Classroom Integration

Before starting this activity, discuss compass points (north, south, east, and west) with the students. Explain how compasses work and also how the sun can be used to determine direction. Mark the walls of the gym and school with N, S, E, and W.

▶*Pedometer Frisbee® Golf*

Frisbee golf is similar to regular golf, except that Frisbees are thrown rather than golf balls hit. Pedometers can give the game a different twist. In this variation, students play regular Frisbee golf; however, scorekeeping rules are different. High and low individual step counts and high and low group step counts are used to determine the winner of the match.

Purpose

1. To learn the basic rules of golf

a

Checkpoint	Landmark	Number of steps	Letter
1	Monkey bars	175-200	A
2	Flagpole	60-85	Y
3	Parking lot gate	250-275	I
4	Front door of gym	150-175	T
5	Door of room 9	100-125	C
6	Drinking fountain	300-325	V
7	Basketball court	160-185	T
8	Trash can by principal's office	125-150	I

b

Take 125 steps NE toward marker 5.

Proceed 85 steps S around the slide to marker 2.

Walk backward in a SW direction for 110 steps to marker 1.

Jog 75 steps N to marker 3.

Skip SW 140 steps to marker 4.

Take 75 steps NE toward the slide. From this point, jog 25 steps W to marker 6.

Slide 45 times NW toward marker 8.

Marker 7 is 85 steps SE of marker 8.

Figure 5.3 Samples of orienteering directions. *(a)* Beginner course with visual landmarks. *(b)* Intermediate course with directions. See page 73 for more information about the use of the letters in the figure.

2. To play the game with an emphasis on step counts rather than Frisbee throws

Activity Description

1. Teach the students the rules of Frisbee golf. Post a rules sign and course map at each tee box. See figure 5.4 for a list of rules that can be used to teach students the basics of regulation golf.

2. Boundary cones with numbers are used for tees, and holes are marked with boxes, hula hoops, trees, tires, trash cans, or any other available equipment on the school grounds. Areas around swings and slides can be designated bunkers or out of bounds. Weather permitting, parachutes and mats can also be used as hazards. Draw a course on a map and provide a copy for every three or four students (see figure 5.5 for an example). Start the groups at different holes to decrease the time spent waiting to tee off. Once a course is established, laminating the maps increases their longevity. Over time, several courses can be created and alternated.

Frisbee golf is played like regular golf. One stroke is counted each time the disk is thrown or when a penalty is incurred. The object of the game is to acquire the lowest score. The following rules dictate play.

- *Tee throws:* Tee throws must be completed within or behind the designated tee area.
- *Lie:* The lie is the spot on or directly underneath the spot where the previous throw landed.
- *Throwing order:* The player whose disk is the farthest from the hole throws first. The player with the least number of throws on the previous hole tees off first.
- *Fairway throws:* Fairway throws must be made with the foot closest to the hole on the lie. A run-up is allowed.
- *Dogleg:* A dogleg is one or more designated trees or poles in the fairway that must be passed on the outside when approaching the hole.
- *Putt throw:* A putt throw is any throw within 10 feet of the hole. A player may not move past the point of the lie in making the putt throw. Falling or jumping putts are not allowed.
- *Unplayable lies:* Any disk that comes to rest 6 feet or move above the ground is unplayable. The next throw must be played from a new lie directly underneath the unplayable lie (one-stroke penalty).
- *Out of bounds:* A throw that lands out of bounds must be played from the point at which the disk went out (one-stroke penalty).
- *Course courtesy:* Do not throw until the players ahead are out of range.
- *Completion of hole:* A disk coming to rest in the hole (box or hoop) or striking the designated hole (tree or pole) constitutes successful completion of that hole.

Figure 5.4   Frisbee golf rules.

3. Explain the basics of Frisbee golf to the students: "Every throw counts as a stroke and the object is to get all the way around the course with as few strokes as possible." Keep the game simple by making hazards count as one stroke.

4. Discuss golf etiquette with the students, including "playing through" and waiting for a group to putt out.

5. Give each student a pedometer and a Frisbee. Reset the pedometer as soon as it is fastened in proper position. As the students play the course, give feedback and randomly check step counts.

6. Determine match winners based on the following:
   - Highest individual step count

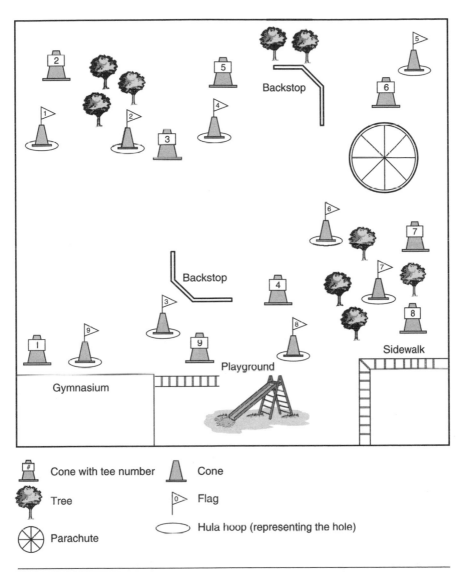

Figure 5.5 Frisbee golf course.

- Lowest individual step count (It can be argued that the person who completes the course with the fewest throws will also take the fewest steps.)
- Highest group step count
- Lowest group step count

▶ Other Golf Activities

Frisbee golf is not the only way to adapt golf and teach other skills. Soccer golf, throwing golf, and rolling golf are all effective games that allow students to practice skills while increasing activity level. These games are played by the same rules as Frisbee golf, with a few exceptions.

Soccer Golf

Soccer golf involves kicking a soccer ball rather than throwing a Frisbee. It is likely that the holes for soccer golf will need to be made longer and larger. Hole size will vary depending on the skill level of the students. An alternative is to use balls that do not travel as well as soccer balls, such as Nerf balls or medium-sized yarn balls, with older students. This alternative allows more holes in a smaller area.

Throwing Golf

Throwing golf is Frisbee golf using a ball rather than a Frisbee. The type of ball used depends on the age of the students and the size of the course. Younger students may be able to use balls such as tennis balls that travel well if the course is rather large. A Wiffle ball or small yarn ball is better for older students because they can throw the ball farther.

Rolling Golf

Rolling golf can be played with a variety of balls depending on the size of the course and age of the students. An alternative for all of the golf games is to allow students to shoot two rounds under different conditions and compare their step counts for each round. For example, allow third graders to play throwing golf with a tennis ball and then with a Wiffle ball. After the second round, discuss why step counts may be greater for one round than the other. Another example is to compare a round of Frisbee golf with a round of soccer golf.

▶ Pedometer Scavenger Hunt

ENGLISH, HISTORY, GEOGRAPHY, MATH

Scavenger hunts using pedometers offer an enjoyable activity that promotes physical activity and integration. Numerous hunts can be created to add variety and excitement to lessons while encouraging students to move.

Purpose

1. To provide students with a fun way to accumulate physical activity

2. To integrate other academic areas into physical education

Activity Description

1. Set up a course similar to the one described in the orienteering section.

2. Place an envelope at each marker with an index card for each group (laminating these cards will improve their longevity). As was done with orienteering (see figure 5.3), provide a landmark, direction, and distance on each index card, but add a clue to a puzzle that must be solved. This puzzle can be a word, a picture, or a statement, depending on the age level of the students. For example, if eight markers are used, each card could contain two of the following letters PH, YS, IC, AL, AC, TI, VI, and TY. Once all markers have been visited, the students would have eight cards that must be unscrambled to spell PHYSICAL ACTIVITY.

Variations

1. To add difficulty, scramble the letters (e.g., PY, IC, AL, TV, II, SH, AY, TC). In this variation, the two letters on the card do not necessarily go side by side in the solution PHYSICAL ACTIVITY.

2. Cut pictures into eight pieces and paste the pieces on index cards to create a puzzle.

3. Create a puzzle with a physical activity theme to reinforce the concept of lifestyle activity.

Classroom Integration

The puzzle can also integrate other subject areas into physical education. The following ideas for integration could be considered when developing clues and puzzles.

1. Class spelling words for the week

2. Characteristics of a country, state, or city the class has studied

3. Numbers and math symbols that make a math problem

4. Pictures of coins (or fake coins) that must be added to determine a total

5. Words that describe a specific animal

6. Descriptions of books the class has read

7. Pictures of national monuments or landmarks that have been cut into puzzle pieces

▶Pedometer Sport Activities

Pedometers can add a different spin to sport activities. Traditionally, sports are designed in a manner that favors the gifted students, making the less-gifted students inactive participants. By incorporating step counts into a sport, accumulating physical activity becomes the focus of the sport as opposed to athletic ability. Pedometers also allow students to understand how much activity they receive from different sports, and teachers can see how active their students are during sport units or lessons. The following are examples of sports that can be modified slightly to focus on physical activity and increase the number of steps students accumulate during play.

Alaskan Softball

Arrange the students on the field and at bat as shown in figure 5.6. After hitting (off a tee, self-tossed, or pitched) or throwing the ball, the batter runs around his or her team, who are standing in a single-file line. Each time the batter comes to the front of the line, the team gets a point. The modification that increases activity is that the point only counts if the whole team is running or jumping in place and cheering for the batter.

While the batter is running, the fielding team must run to the student who fields the ball, make a single-file line behind the fielder while running in place, and pass the ball to the end of the line, alternating over the head and between the legs. When the ball gets to the end of the line, the team yells, "Stop!" The batter then stops running, and only completed laps count for the batting team's points. Rotate the teams between field and batting after five to seven students have batted.

Speed Softball

This game is played by groups of four or five students. Each player tries to see how many runs he or she can score. Players include a catcher, a batter, a pitcher, and one or two fielders as positioned in figure 5.7. The batter chooses how the ball will be put into play (off a tee, self-tossed, a hit pitch, or thrown). Once the ball is in play, the batter begins running back and forth between home plate and a base located where second base would be on a regular softball diamond. The running distance will vary depending on the age level and skill of the students. Each time the batter touches home plate, a point is scored. While the batter runs between the bases, the fielders, running in place, toss the ball from one to the other and then relay it to the catcher, who is positioned by home plate. When the catcher steps on the plate with the ball in hand, the fielders yell, "Stop!" Only completed laps between bases count as runs for the batter.

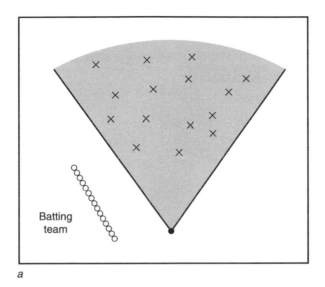

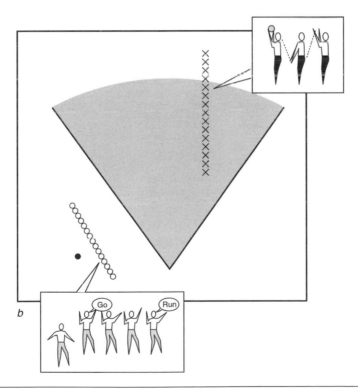

Figure 5.6 Alaskan softball. *(a)* Overhead view of the playing field before the ball is put into play. *(b)* Overhead view of the playing field after the ball is put into play.

The players then rotate so everyone gets a chance to play every position. To encourage quick rotations, the catcher rotates to batter and puts the ball in play as soon as it is safe to do so. Because the new batter will already be at home plate, this rotation will require all players to hustle to their next position (see the rotation in figure 5.7). Each player's runs, or points, accumulate from one at bat to the next. At the end of the game each player adds his or her step counts to his or her runs for a total score. This system provides an incentive for students to be active and makes steps more important than runs.

Sideline Basketball

Sideline basketball is an active lead-up game for students. Facing each other, teams line up on the sidelines of the court. Sideline players must run or jump in place during the game. At the start of the game, four players from each team enter the court and play regulation basketball. Players on the court can pass the ball to sideline players, but sideline players cannot move along the sideline or shoot the ball. Sideline players can pass to each other if they wish, but no more than three passes are permitted before the ball must be passed back to players on the court. After one minute of play, court players quickly join the sideline players at the left end of the line and the next four players enter the court from the right. The remaining sideline players spread out to cover the entire sideline. The only out of bounds are the end lines, and free throws are granted if a player is fouled while shooting. Scoring is based on points scored and total steps at the end of the game.

Horse

This traditional game is easily adapted to increase the activity level of all participants. All nonshooters can jog or slide (defensive) around the area until it is their turn to shoot. In addition, all players can actively rebound the ball and quickly pass it to the next shooter. At the end of the game, the player with the fewest letters receives 250 bonus steps, and the player with the most steps is the winner. This strategy rewards steps rather than skill. An alternative is to allow students to play a game with the pedometers on, write down their step counts, and then introduce the new scoring system where accumulating steps is more important than winning the game. The student who shows the biggest increase in step count from the first game to the second game is the overall winner. This scoring system gives all students an opportunity to succeed.

Football Lead-Up Games

Traditionally, football involves brief periods of vigorous activity followed by long periods of inactivity before the next play. Therefore, traditional football

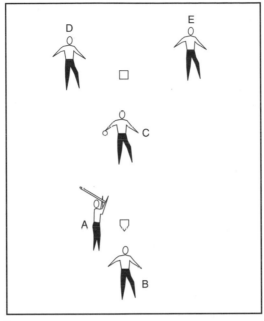

Figure 5.7 Speed softball. *(a)* First rotation and *(b)* second rotation.

is not generally thought of as a lifestyle activity. However, having teams walk or jog in place between plays makes it a much more active game.

An alternative is to play fanatical football. This game is a nonstop hybrid of football, team handball, and ultimate Frisbee. Team A kicks (or throws) off to team B. Team B then attempts to move the ball toward their end zone. When downed (tagged or flagged), the player with the ball instantly (without waiting for the line of scrimmage to set up) becomes the quarterback and looks to pass the ball to a teammate (the pass can be forward or backward). The quarterback cannot be rushed and cannot run more than three steps. Once a pass is completed to a teammate, the receiver can run with the ball until downed, and then he or she becomes the quarterback. This process continues until team B scores a touchdown, team A intercepts, or team B makes an incomplete pass. If team B scores, they immediately turn and kick off. The player who scores is not eligible to kick off, and they do not wait for team A to walk. If team A intercepts, the interceptor immediately becomes the quarterback and his or her team moves toward their end zone. If team B makes an incomplete pass, the member of team A closest to the ball becomes the quarterback and the game continues. To ensure that everyone on the team is involved, keep teams small, use more than one ball, or make a rule that all team members must touch the ball before a team can score.

Scoring can be altered to include step counts in football or football lead-up games. All the students wear pedometers, but each team has one pedometer that is rotated among team members. This extra pedometer is the pedometer used to track steps as points. The pedometer is rotated to allow all students to feel as if they have contributed to the team. A quick rotation takes place at time intervals or after each score. At the end of the game, to emphasize activity and not touchdowns, add team step counts and team scores to find the team with the most points. These modifications offer simple continuous alternatives to traditional football and allow students to accumulate a substantial number of steps.

Line Soccer

Line soccer is a sport lead-up game that can be modified to increase the amount of physical activity opportunities. Students are divided into two teams and set up as shown in figure 5.8. The setup and play are the same as sideline basketball (see page 76), with a few exceptions. The obvious exceptions are that soccer rules are used rather than basketball rules and players are spread out along the endlines as well as the sidelines. Players on the sidelines and endlines are goalies, who must prevent balls from going through their line. Nerf balls are used instead of regulation soccer balls, and only balls that travel through the line of goalies below

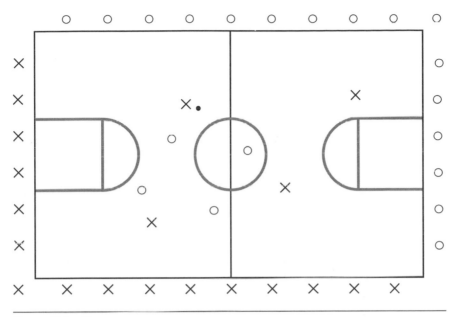

Figure 5.8 Line soccer.

chest height are considered goals. To increase activity, all players serv-ing as goalies (sideline and endline players) have to walk or jog in place. More than one ball can be used (no more than three or four for safety reasons) to increase activity levels. A variation is to award two bonus goals for the team that has the most steps at the end of the game, or this could be included as part of the regular game.

Pedometer Enhanced Relays

Relay races can be adapted to increase activity level. Traditionally, team members who are finished with their legs of the relay stand or sit until the race is over. A way to increase activity in any relay race is to have the waiting team members and finished team members jump and cheer for the runners. The following are examples of relays that require movement by all team members throughout the race. Students can first participate in a traditional relay race while wearing pedometers, then run one of the relays presented below. Afterward, the students can discuss which method accumulates the most activity.

Kangaroo Relay

Student A, holding a 36-inch wand with two hands, runs to the desig-nated area and back. When he or she gets back to the line, student B

Kangaroo relay.

grabs one end of the wand, with student A holding the other end. Keeping the wand about 12 inches (30 centimeters) off of the ground, they move down the line of teammates, allowing each team member to jump the wand. At the end of the line, student B, while holding the wand in front with two hands, runs to the designated area and back. Student B and student C hold the wand and move down the line of teammates, again with each team member jumping the wand. This process is repeated until all team members have carried the wand down and back one time.

Chain Relay

Student A in each team runs to the designated turning point and back. Student A then joins hands with student B, and they both run down and back. Student B then joins hands with student C, and all three run down and back together. This process continues until the entire team joins hands and runs down and back.

Hoop and Go Relay

Student A runs down and back carrying a hoop. The entire team then joins hands and passes the hoop to the end of the line by going through the hoop. When the hoop gets to the end of the line, the last student runs down and back, and the team must pass through the hoop with hands joined. The race proceeds until all team members have carried the hoop down and back.

Pass and Squat Relay

Team members are in lane formation with players standing 7 to 10 feet (2 to 3 meters) apart. Student 1 faces the rest of the team when the relay begins. Student 1 passes the ball to student 2, who quickly passes the ball back to student 1 and then squats. Student 1 now passes the ball to student 3, who passes it back and squats. Passing and squatting continue until the last student in line receives the ball. This student carries the ball to the front of the line and becomes the passer while all other students move back one place. The race is over when student 1 receives the ball at the back of the line and returns to his or her original position.

Attention Relay

Teams are in lane formation at least two arm's lengths apart. Team members are 7 to 10 feet (2 to 3 meters) apart. Turning points are designated 10 feet (3 meters) in front of the lane and 10 feet (3 meters) behind the lane. All students are assigned a number, starting at the front of the line. When the teacher calls, "Attention!" all students assume a military-style attention position. The teacher then calls out a number. The student from each team assigned that number steps to the right, runs around the front and back turning points, and returns to his or her original space while the rest of the team runs in place. The first team to have the runner and all other members at attention gets the point.

Extracurricular Activities

Many schools offer before-school, after-school, and lunch-hour programs for students. These extracurricular activities include clubs, intramural sports, and before- and after-school programs that provide students with a safe place to stay before school or before being picked up by their parents after school. An opportune time to promote lifestyle activity, the following are ideas for extracurricular activities or programs that use pedometers to promote physical activity.

▶Physical Activity Clubs

Physical activity clubs (PACs) promote lifestyle activity by making physical activity fun for all students. Like walking clubs and intramural clubs, PACs can be conducted before and after school, as well as during recess.

Using pedometers, students can track their physical activity during a given period and record their step counts on their own PAC sheets (see form 5.1 for an example).

Purpose

1. To provide students with an opportunity to measure their physical activity level using a pedometer
2. To promote lifestyle activity
3. To establish a club that all students are encouraged to join
4. To demonstrate to students that all activity is important regardless of the intensity or type

Activity Description

1. Meet with the principal to discuss options for a possible PAC.
2. Brainstorm with other teachers about the PAC.
3. Advertise the program around the school using catchy slogans such as, "Join the PAC," or "Come be a part of the PAC."
4. Design PAC sheets for recording step counts.
5. Speak with local businesspeople about possible donations for PAC shirts or pedometers.
6. Create a schedule for pedometer use. For example, Mrs. Hernandez's class gets the pedometers at recess on Monday and Tuesday, and Mr. O'Connor's class uses them after school on Monday and Wednesday.
7. Discuss the PAC with all classes. Emphasize that it includes all activities.
8. Establish a location for PAC sheets to be stored and pedometers to be returned. The students should record their step counts and return the pedometers to the same location at the same time.
9. Appoint students as "pedometer police" for each class. These students are responsible for making sure all pedometers have been returned after the activity period. Give every student an opportunity to serve as a pedometer police officer.
10. Develop ways of promoting the PAC. Possibilities include announcing the names of students who have become PAC members, organizing a charity activity-thon, and providing mini-rewards to students who increase their step counts for a given period.

Teaching Hints

1. Begin with one grade level to ease implementation.
2. At the outset, be visible during activity times. Your presence creates enthusiasm for the program within the school and allows you to maintain quality control.

PAC Step Sheet

Name _____

Teacher _____

Date	Steps

Date	Steps

Date	Steps

Date	Steps

3. Allow students who are not using pedometers for a given day to enter their previous step counts into a spreadsheet and graph their data during this time. Encourage them to do this quickly and remain active, even on the days they do not use the pedometers.

▶PAC Charity Walk/Jog

Charity walks/jogs are very popular and very productive forms of physical activity. By sponsoring a charity walk/jog, the PAC not only promotes lifestyle activity but also gets students involved with charity and doing good deeds for others. Encourage parents to participate in these events as a way of promoting lifestyle activity in the community. During the event, let as many people as possible (students and parents) wear pedometers. If possible, get sponsors to base donations on the number of steps taken by participants.

Purpose

1. To promote physical activity
2. To teach charitable behavior

Activity Description

1. Determine a charity to benefit from the event. Some proceeds could also go toward buying pedometers.
2. Contact the charity representative to discuss your event. This person will be able to provide valuable information regarding promotion, donations, and volunteers to help with the event.
3. Work closely with the charity's personnel to plan the event.
4. At the event, make pedometers available for check out.
5. At the event, give families a list of family-oriented activities (see chapter 7, page 106).

▶PAC Family Fun Day

By sponsoring a Family Fun Day, the PAC can designate a day for students and parents to be active together and monitor their physical activity. This day showcases physical activity, the PAC, and the physical education program. Students can demonstrate their skills as well as show parents the equipment, including pedometers, used during physical education. This day can also become a weekly event. For example, every Saturday morning is made Family Fun Day at the school. The activities could be rotated based on the physical education lessons taught during the week or the interests of the families in attendance.

Purpose

1. To promote lifestyle activity
2. To allow students and parents to use pedometers together
3. To showcase the PAC and the physical education program

Activity Description

1. Determine a date for the event. Set aside an alternative rain date.
2. Send fliers to parents and local businesses. These reminders should be sent several times before the event.
3. Recruit volunteers.
4. Plan activities. Arrange activities around booths, with equipment displayed and areas delineated for playing. This setup allows families to choose and possibly create their activities.
5. Organize activities and volunteers.
6. During the event, allow families to check out pedometers.
7. Also, provide handouts containing information on family activities (see chapter 7) and how to buy pedometers.

▶ PAC Moving Across America

GEOGRAPHY, MATH, HISTORY, ENGLISH

Moving Across America not only can be a physical education activity but also can be a club activity. The major difference is that PAC Moving Across America is used to encourage students to be active on their own time. Students are allowed to accumulate steps before or after school during extracurricular programs and at recesses. Also, if feasible, students can be permitted to check out pedometers to take home (see page 31 for details regarding checking out pedometers). Establish a PAC before introducing Moving Across America to facilitate this program. Open the PAC to all students because all students are capable of being active. Provide adult supervision for this activity, especially in the initial phases.

Purpose

1. To expose students to the value of physical activity
2. To allow students to track their activity and see how much they move
3. To provide students with a safe opportunity to accumulate physical activity

4. To motivate students to be active

5. To integrate physical activity into many academic areas

Activity Description

This activity assumes that a system for checking out pedometers and recording step counts has already been established. First graders may be too young to participate in the program; thus, participants are assumed to be in grades 2 to 6. Before joining a PAC, each student should determine how many of his or her steps equal a mile. See chapter 4, page 50, for details on determining stride length.

1. During physical education class, give a brief (no more than 5 minutes) explanation of the program and how to participate.

2. Hand out a data-recording sheet (see form 5.1) and teach the students how and when to record their steps.

3. Establish a time frame for how often the students will trace their progress on the map. Designate 1 day a week for a "finding where you are" time. For example, every Monday, second graders can calculate their total steps and find their new location. On other days, students in other grades can track their progression across America during their allotted time.

Classroom Integration

Classroom teachers can use the following ideas to integrate PAC Moving Across America into subject areas. These ideas are based on adding the step counts from all students and calculating the total number of miles traveled by the class. A predetermined route can be used to allow teachers to prepare lessons and activities based on where the class is traveling each week. Students can

1. Draw maps of the current location.

2. Discuss the culture of the closest city.

3. Determine how far it is to the next city, state, or landmark.

4. Determine how many steps will be necessary to reach the next area.

5. Write an essay about the current location.

6. Study the history of the closest city.

7. Study the plants, trees, animals, and insects of the current region.

Moving Across America is an ongoing event in which students can accumulate step counts and miles, from the second grade to the sixth grade and beyond if the program is used at the secondary-school level. If sufficient pedometers are available, Moving Across America can also be an out-of-school project, in which students wear pedometers in the evening and add those steps to the steps they accumulate in the PAC at school.

▶Active Intramurals

Lunchtime and after-school intramurals are gaining popularity at elementary schools. The programs provide great opportunities for using pedometers and promoting lifestyle activity. The following is a list of potential methods of emphasizing activity through intramurals.

1. Steps-based scoring. Every student wears a pedometer, and pedometer steps are logged on stat sheets after each game. Game points and accumulated step counts (or average step counts) for a team are totaled, and the team with the highest total wins. In this system, a team could be outscored by 50 points and still win by adding its accumulated step counts to its score.
2. Steps-based awards. Awards based on steps and, if desired, traditional awards based on wins and scoring, can be given. The following step awards can be given for each intramural season.
   - Most Improved Stepper. The student who has the most improved average step count per game wins a prize.
   - Most Valuable Stepper. The student who accumulates the most steps during the intramural season or who averages the most steps per game wins a prize (or a different student can be awarded each prize).
   - The team that averages the most steps per game wins a prize.
   - The team that accumulates the most steps during intramurals wins a prize.
3. Awards based on "activityship" (e.g., awards for encouraging others to be active).

These additions to an intramural program will emphasize physical activity over skill. This philosophy has two purposes: (1) to promote lifestyle activity and teach students the importance of being active regardless of ability and (2) to allow students who are less skilled to contribute to the team and experience success.

▶Schoolwide Pedometer Step Contest

All classrooms in a school can be involved in this contest. The step counts of all students in the class are added and then divided by the number of students. Using the average number of steps eliminates confusion caused by classes of different sizes. This contest is best used within grade levels because of the limited number of pedometers available. For example, all fourth-grade classes compete against each other, and then fifth-grade classes get a turn, and so on. After all classes have collected step counts, an overall school winner can also be determined. There are several methods for setting up the contest.

1. Students and classroom teachers wear the pedometers for one school day. The following day, another class wears the pedometers.

2. Students and classroom teachers wear the pedometers for the entire day, which requires setting a start time. For example, on day 1, students in class A put the pedometers on at 9:00 A.M. if school starts at 8:00 A.M. On day 2, class A brings the pedometers back to school, records their step counts, and leaves the pedometers for class B, who puts them on at 9:00 A.M. Each class follows the same pattern.

3. Students and classroom teachers wear the pedometers all day Monday through Thursday. Tuesday through Friday morning, step counts are recorded, and the pedometers are returned to you on Friday morning. This schedule gives you time to prepare the pedometers for the next Monday morning class.

This chapter offers numerous activity ideas for using pedometers in elementary physical education. These activities not only help children understand their own physical activity, they also teach children to think about physical activity and the amount of physical activity offered by a variety of activities. Many of the activities presented also serve to allow physical education teachers to integrate other subject areas into the physical education curriculum with minimal interruptions. By using the ideas presented in this chapter, as well as ideas that are generated through their own experiences, teachers can promote lifestyle physical activity for all children through the use of pedometers.

If You Want to Know More . . .

The following list of Web sites and references will provide teachers with supplemental materials related to promoting physical activity for elementary students. These resources include lesson ideas, ideas for teaching health concepts to children, research and information regarding physical activity and elementary age children, and programs promoting developmentally appropriate sports for children.

Web Sites

www.cdc.gov
The Web site of the Centers for Disease Control and Prevention.

http://sunsite.berkeley.edu/KidsClick!
This search engine for children was constructed by librarians. Children can use it to learn about physical activity. In particular, check out the section titled "Health & Family."

www.learn-orienteering.org
This site provides ideas for orienteering lessons (e.g., How to Use a Compass).

www.sports-media.org
Physical Education & Sports for Everyone. This site offers lesson plans, interactive discussions on physical education activities, and related links.

http://reach.ucf.edu/%7Epezone/home.html
PE Zone is a resource for teachers and educators interested in promoting health, physical education, and wellness.

www.education-world.com
This site is the educator's best friend. It provides a searchable database of over 100,000 education links for teachers, parents, and students (see specific article on physical activity listed in "Article," next page).

www.healthfinder.gov/kids
The Web site provided by the Office of Disease Prevention and Health Promotion, U.S. Department of Health and Human Services (offers ways for children to be healthy and have fun).

www.ops.org/pe/elem.html
Elementary Physical Education Page of the Omaha Public Schools. This site provides sample activities in which the pedometer can be incorporated.

www.directcon.net/spring4/index.html
This Web site is designed and maintained by a school nurse/health educator from Sacramento, California. Visitors to the site can get integrated health lesson ideas (with math, social studies, etc.).

www.foundation.sdsu.edu/projects/spark/index.html
SPARK (Sports, Play, and Active Recreation for Kids) is an elementary physical education program that began as a National Institute of Health research grant. SPARK is a nonprofit organization of San Diego State University dedicated to improving physical education for children and teachers everywhere.

www.hearteheart.com
A health and lifestyle curriculum for students in grades 1 to 3 that includes 10 cartoon characters designed to convey complex physiologic functions to teach children about exercise, nutrition, and safety.

www.sportforall.net
SPORT FOR ALL is a new program that provides developmentally appropriate uses of sport-related skills for children 3 to 10 years of age to start them on a path to regular, lifelong physical activity.

Article

Hopkins, G. 1998. Let's get physical! *Education World.* **www.education-world.com/ a_lesson/lesson063.shtml**

Reference

Pangrazi, R.P. 2001. *Dynamic physical education for elementary school children (13th ed.)*. Boston: Allyn and Bacon.

Pedometer Activities for Secondary School Students

Mr. Sonjay and Mrs. Matulevich were discussing how to make their students at Mountview Junior High School aware of the benefits of physical activity and fitness. Mr. Sonjay is a relatively new teacher with 3 years of experience, whereas Mrs. Matulevich is a veteran with 20 years of experience.

Mr. Sonjay: I think heart rate monitors are the way to go with students once they get to junior high. Kids need to learn about target heart range and fitness.

Mrs. Matulevich: Yes, heart rate monitors can be very useful, but remember we're focusing on lifestyle activity for health. Besides, if we want to teach students about target heart rate, we can teach them about how to take their pulse rate and calculate their training zone. This may be more practical for them anyway since most of them won't have access to a heart rate monitor outside of physical education class. I think pedometers make more sense.

Mr. Sonjay: But aren't pedometers just little gadgets to trick elementary students into being active. They won't work with older kids.

Mrs. Matulevich: We can use pedometers in the secondary curricu-lum, too. At this level, physical education should be preparing students to head out into the real world. Getting them involved in lifestyle activity is very important. Just like with other new activities, we can start with something simple, such as having the students wear pedometers during physical education class. From there, we can develop ideas and create activities as we go.

This chapter describes pedometer activities that can be easily imple-mented in a secondary physical education curriculum. After participat-ing in a quality elementary physical education program, the logical progression for students is to begin making their own decisions regard-ing physical activity and thinking about the outcomes of specific activi-ties. The activities presented in this chapter are designed to achieve these goals. Also, it should be noted that most activities presented in chapter 5 can be adapted for secondary school students as well.

Physical Education Pedometer Activities

The activities in this chapter are designed to help students develop an understanding about the relationship between physical activity and different activities. Emphasis is placed on students designing and modi-fying games and sports to maximize their physical activity potential. Another important set of activities teaches students how to measure their baseline level of activity and how to set meaningful activity goals.

▶ Student-Modified Activities Based on Pedometer Steps

This lesson is useful for teaching students that it is possible to change their activity behavior in a variety of settings to increase the benefits received from physical activity.

Purpose

1. To teach students about physical activity by allowing them to use pedometers to monitor steps
2. To encourage students to think about ways to change activities to increase physical activity

Activity Description

1. Have the students wear pedometers during any physical education lesson and record their steps at the end of the lesson.

2. During their next physical education lesson, challenge the students to create ways in which the same lesson can be made more active.

3. Provide the following guidelines for the activities:
   - The activities must be safe.
   - The activities must be at an intensity level that all students can achieve.
   - The activities must get everyone involved. For example, the students may allow only one bounce in volleyball games to lengthen rallies and decrease the time players stand still or modify the rules of traditional softball to increase the activity level of the game.

4. Using pedometers, students can then test the impact of their new rules on their step counts.

▶ Student-Developed Activities

Another strategy for stimulating junior high or high school students to think about physical activity is to have them invent their own games, which may result in new activities that you can use in other classes (see figure 6.1).

Figure 6.1   Students inventing a game.

Purpose

1. To allow students to use pedometers to monitor their physical activity level during unique activities
2. To have students create their own ways of being active
3. To encourage cooperation

Activity Description

1. Scatter sets of equipment around the teaching area. One set may be a Nerf ball, a cone, a softball glove, and a jump rope. Another set may be a scooter, a playground ball, and a compass.
2. Let the students organize themselves into groups of four to six, all wearing pedometers.
3. Allow each group to pick one set of equipment.
4. Instruct the groups to invent games in which they use the equipment and apply the following rules:
   - The game must be safe.
   - Everyone must be active and participate in the game.
   - The equipment must be used in an acceptable, but not necessarily traditional, manner.
   - Add a challenge by requiring that at least one piece of equipment be used in a manner different from its traditional use (e.g., using a racket to catch rather than strike a ball).
5. Give the groups 15 to 20 minutes to create and play the games while monitoring their steps. They may find it necessary to make changes based on the steps accumulated during play.
6. During subsequent lessons, again give the groups the opportunity to play their games for a set amount of time and monitor their steps. However, during these lessons, focus on sharing activities with the class or other groups.
7. Discuss why some games may be more active than others.
8. Discuss why a group or a student may be more active during one game than another group or student.

Student-Designed Pedometer Orienteering Course

In chapter 5, we described a teacher-designed pedometer orienteering course. Because the goal in secondary physical education is to encourage students to be become responsible for their activity and to teach them to make appropriate decisions regarding their physical activity, students design their own orienteering course.

Purpose

1. To teach students to use a pedometer as a tool for both assessing physical activity and aiding in orienteering
2. To provide students with experience in designing and navigating their own orienteering course
3. To show students the importance of cooperation

Activity Description

1. Create a blank map of the school grounds or other area used for orienteering, with boundaries clearly marked. The orienteering area should be safe from any hazards.
2. Design a course and introduce orienteering (see figures 5.2 and 5.3, pp. 68 and 69, for details). Depending on school policy, the area used for orienteering can be on or off school property.
3. During the initial lesson, let the students know that they will design a course for their group and that other groups will use their course. This knowledge will ensure that they carefully monitor their steps, which will give them an idea of the number of steps required during orienteering. Discuss how to develop instructions and place markers.
4. During the ensuing lessons, divide the class into groups of three or four students, and give them time to map out their courses and to create instructions and place markers. Have the students draw their maps on blank maps of the area. This procedure may require two or three lessons, depending on the area. However, because the students walk to create and then follow their courses, they are active.
5. Have the students estimate the number of steps required and then test their estimation to determine the actual number of steps to be placed on the map.
6. Once all groups have finished their courses and recorded the approximate number of required steps, collect the maps and read them to ensure clarity of instructions. This quality control prevents embarrassment and ridicule from peers when maps are exchanged.
7. Have the students exchange maps and attempt to navigate the courses created by other groups. Groups use the instructions provided by the mapmakers to navigate the course.
8. Have the students compare the number of steps taken by the other groups with their count. Discuss factors that can influence step counts (i.e., stride length, cutting corners).

9. Add a challenge by asking the students to design a course that will take approximately 2,500 steps or to create a course that will be approximately 1 mile (1.6 kilometers). For consistency, groups can designate one member as the "stepper" for measuring distance. See page 50 for details on measuring stride length.

▶ *Activity Exploration* ENGLISH

Activity exploration not only allows students to reflect on their activity but also provides them with a chance to experience a variety of activities, many of which students may have never tried otherwise.

Purpose

1. To encourage students to participate in new activities
2. To teach students how to monitor the number of steps accumulated during a variety of activities
3. To allow students to express their findings and thoughts through writing

Activity Description

1. Discuss lifestyle activity and its importance with the students (refer to page 3). Allow the class to brainstorm and think of activities that can be classified as lifestyle activities.
2. Explain that each student will wear a pedometer while participating in two lifestyle activities and one activity must be something in which the student has never participated.
3. After the students have participated in each activity for the same amount of time (20 to 30 minutes), allow them to record their step counts.
4. Ask the students to write a one-page paper that includes the following:
   - An explanation of the activities and why they are lifestyle activities
   - The amount of steps accumulated while participating in the activities
   - Whether one activity was better than the other and why
   - Why the student did or did not enjoy each activity

▶ *Peer Teaching*

Most would agree that teaching an activity helps ensure a better understanding of the activity. Peer teaching is effective in a class after students have developed the independence and self-discipline to work on their own.

Purpose

1. To encourage students to think of a variety of lifestyle activities
2. To expose students to teaching lifestyle activities
3. To provide students with numerous options for lifestyle activities and an understanding of the amount of activity they provide

Activity Description

1. Discuss lifestyle activities with the class, including examples.
2. Assign students to present, or teach, lifestyle activities to the class or a small group. Activities in which the class or group can participate during physical education are desired. However, if the physical education program does not have the equipment or facilities, the activity can be presented and discussed without participation.
3. After the students teach or present the activities, have them lead the groups or classes in the activities for 10 minutes while everyone wears pedometers.
4. Document the steps accumulated during each activity on cards (see page 27).
5. Discuss the effectiveness of the activities and ways to modify them to increase physical activity levels. Allow the students to test the effectiveness of their suggestions for increasing physical activity levels.
6. After the students have presented their activities, list all activities along with the number of steps accumulated in 10 minutes. The students can take this information home or place it in their portfolios.

The following series of activities should first be done in physical education classes. Once students become familiar with the activities, they can be given the option of using pedometers to measure these activities inside and outside of school daily. For details about checking out pedometers, see chapter 3, page 31.

▶Establishing Baseline Step Counts for Daily Physical Activity

This activity forms the foundation for many of the activities that follow. It is important to know what your baseline step count is if you are going to set personal physical activity goals that have meaning.

Purpose

1. To allow students to monitor their own daily physical activity level using pedometers and establish their average daily step counts
2. To encourage students to be active

Activity Description

1. Give each student a step-count data sheet similar to form 6.1. This sheet will also be used for Goal Setting Using a Pedometer and Individual Intervention Programs that follow.
2. Encourage the students to track their step counts for 4 days and calculate their average daily physical activity.

▶Goal Setting Using a Pedometer

Goals have to be reasonable and personal if they are going to make changes in your daily habits. Pedometers are useful for increasing physical activity because they reveal how much activity you are accumulating on a day-to-day basis.

Purpose

1. To teach students the process of goal setting
2. To encourage students to be physically active
3. To teach students how to use pedometers to monitor their progress toward goals
4. To allow students to be successful and reach realistic goals

Activity Description

1. During physical education class, briefly discuss goal setting with step counts. See chapter 2 for a discussion of goal setting.
2. Instruct the students to use the average number of steps generated during self-monitoring to set achievable goals for themselves.
3. Have the students check their progress toward their goals each time they use pedometers and make adjustments accordingly.

▶Individual Intervention Programs

Students can develop individual intervention programs (IIPs) based on their baseline data and corresponding goals. Essentially, an IIP is a plan of action for increasing their accumulated physical activity. An outside-

Baseline and Goal-Setting Logs

Baseline Physical Activity Level

Trials	Day 1	Day 2	Day 3	Day 4	Total steps/4 days
1					
2					

Average daily steps

Goal Setting

Average daily steps	Goal (percentage increase)	Goal (step counts)

Individual Intervention Program

Trials	Day 1	Day 2	Day 3	Day 4	Total steps/4 days
1					
2					

New average daily steps

To calculate the percentage change:

[(New average daily steps − Average daily steps) ÷ Average daily steps] × 100 = Percentage change

From *Pedometer Power: 67 Lessons for K–12* by Robert P. Pangrazi, Aaron Beighle, and Cara L. Sidman, 2003, Champaign, IL: Human Kinetics.

of-school IIP may include walking to school or simply spending more time outside during the evening. This activity assumes students have already established their baseline step counts and have set challenging yet achievable goals.

Purpose

1. To introduce students to IIPs
2. To teach students to plan for physical activity
3. To allow students to use pedometers to assess the effectiveness of their IIPs

Activity Description

1. During physical education class, discuss physical activity IIPs. Emphasize that IIPs are essentially just plans for increasing physical activity. For example, rather than sitting for the entire lunch period, students can walk and talk with friends to increase physical activity. Provide examples of interventions that can take place both during physical education class and outside of school (see figure 6.2).
2. Instruct each student to develop his or her own intervention program.
3. Allow the students to use pedometers and their baseline step counts to test the effectiveness of their IIPs.

- Do chores 3 days per week rather than 1 day per week.

- Walk the dog every day.

- Play physically active games or walk rather than sit when you are given free time at school (lunchtime or break time).

- Play with a hacky sack.

- Go for a hike with your parents.

- Rake yards or shovel driveways in your neighborhood.

- Start a family basketball game.

- Walk to school rather than have a parent drive you (with parents' permission).

- Invent dances or dance routines and practice them.

- Organize a physical activity group in your neighborhood, and play a different game or activity each day.

- Play Frisbee or Frisbee golf.

- Snowboard or sled.

Figure 6.2   Intervention strategies.

4. Ask the students to write short papers explaining why they think their IIPs were or were not effective.

5. Encourage the students to continue items 1 to 3 to find a method that works for them.

▶Hypothesis Testing With Pedometers   SCIENCE, ENGLISH

Using pedometers to integrate the scientific process and physical education is simple. Hypothesis testing is a way to reinforce a classroom concept during physical education with minimal interference in the goal of promoting lifestyle activity. The following activity is described for individual students working alone, but students can also work with partners or in small groups if desired.

Purpose

1. To reinforce the scientific process through physical education
2. To teach students to think critically about physical activity

Activity Description

1. Briefly review the scientific process, or hypothesis testing, with the class.

2. Show the students how pedometers can be used for hypothesis testing. For example, pedometers can be used to answer the following questions:
   - Do athletes take more steps during football practice or volleyball practice?
   - Do students take more steps during an orienteering lesson or during a football lesson?
   - Are students more active than parents?

3. Assign students into small groups. Have the students submit questions and corresponding methods for answering the questions using pedometers. Review the assignments for feasibility and appropriateness.

4. Once the projects are approved for each group, allow them to check out one or two pedometers to carry out their tests.

5. After they have completed their tests, each group is responsible for turning in a paper explaining their projects and what they learned.

▶Going for the Guidelines

Given the guidelines for adolescent activity in chapter 1, page 7, students will immediately ask, "How many steps do I take in 30 to 60 minutes?"—a perfect segue into using pedometers during physical education and outside of physical education. Before performing this activity, students should be reminded that these guidelines are the *minimum* recommendations.

Purpose

1. To teach students the physical activity guidelines
2. To see how many steps can be accumulated in 30 to 60 minutes

Activity Description

1. Create a handout using the guidelines for adolescent activity in chapter 1, page 7, to give to students as a reminder.
2. Discuss the guidelines and how they can be used.
3. Have the students use pedometers to record their step counts during a 30-minute (or approximately 30-minute) lesson.
4. Discuss whether this technique is a good way to determine the number of steps taken in 30 minutes. If the students do not think the type of activity is a factor, discuss how the type and intensity of activity can influence the number of steps taken.
5. Continue items 3 and 4 for several lessons. With varied lessons (basketball, orienteering, tennis), students will begin to understand that the number of steps taken can vary depending on the activity, but even walking (e.g., walking during an orienteering lesson) offers a substantial amount of steps in 30 minutes.

If You Want to Know More . . .

The following are examples of the numerous Web sites and other resources available for secondary physical education teachers. These resources offer supplemental information to enhance teaching and improve curricula.

Web Sites

www.sph.uth.tmc.edu/chppr/catch/default.htm
This is the CATCH (Coordinated Approach to Child Health) Web site, dedicated to helping educators, administrators, and parents promote and maintain heart-healthy behaviors in children and adoles-

cents (formerly, The Child and Adolescent Trial for Cardiovascular Health).

www.ops.org/pe/sec.html
Secondary Physical Education: Department of Curriculum and Learning. This Web site provides links for information on a variety of activities.

www.pecentral.org/booksmusic/bookstore/books/secondarytexts.html
This site provides a comprehensive list of secondary physical education books.

Article

Prusak, K. and P. Darst. 2002. Effects of types of walking activities on actual choices by adolescent female physical education students. *Journal of Teaching in Physical Education* 21:230–41.

Books

Darst, P.W. and R.P. Pangrazi. 2001. *Dynamic physical education for secondary school students (4th ed.)*. San Francisco: Benjamin Cummings.

Decker, J. and M. Mize. 2002. *Walking games and activities*. Champaign, IL: Human Kinetics.

McCracken, B. 2001. *It's not just gym anymore: Teaching secondary school students how to be active for life*. Champaign, IL: Human Kinetics.

Pedometer Activities for Families

Arianna: Mom, can you sign this permission slip so that I can wear a pedometer home from school?

Mrs. Fraustino: What's a pedometer?

Arianna: It's this little thing you can wear on your belt, and it counts your steps. Remember, I told you we're using them in physical education class? Now we can borrow one to bring home if we want.

Mrs. Fraustino: You just wear it?

Arianna: You and Dad can wear it, too. The teacher said we should all wear it and see how active we are.

Mrs. Fraustino: Why do I need to know how active I am?

Arianna: So you'll know if you're active enough to stay healthy. All that stuff is in the letter. Don't you and Dad want to be healthy? The teacher said she'll be sending home a list of things we can do with the pedometers.

Mrs. Fraustino: Okay, we'll give it a try.

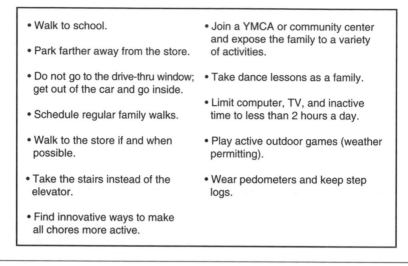

- Walk to school.

- Park farther away from the store.

- Do not go to the drive-thru window; get out of the car and go inside.

- Schedule regular family walks.

- Walk to the store if and when possible.

- Take the stairs instead of the elevator.

- Find innovative ways to make all chores more active.

- Join a YMCA or community center and expose the family to a variety of activities.

- Take dance lessons as a family.

- Limit computer, TV, and inactive time to less than 2 hours a day.

- Play active outdoor games (weather permitting).

- Wear pedometers and keep step logs.

Figure 7.1   General ways to increase family activity.

This chapter presents some family activities that illustrate how to use pedometers to increase the physical activity level of all family members (see figure 7.1). These ideas could be used in a newsletter or on a pedometer use permission slip (see chapter 4) sent home with students. Families can be influential in promoting lifestyle activity outside of school. Thus, methods for increasing family activity levels have the potential to promote lifestyle activity in students (Brustad 1993, 1996; Kimiecik and Horn 1998; Freedson and Evenson 1991).

▶ Pass the Pedometer

This activity can be used by a family when walking the dog, participating in a charity walk, or any other family event that involves physical activity.

Purpose

1. To promote family activity
2. To make family members aware of their activity levels

Activity Description

1. Every 5 to 10 minutes, the person wearing the pedometer looks at the step counts and then passes it to another family member. Other family members guess how many steps were taken.
2. The next family member wears the pedometer for 5 to 10 minutes and the process continues. Each time, the family guesses either the

total accumulated steps by everyone or the steps accumulated by the last person who wore the pedometer.

3. During or after the outing, the family can celebrate their total step counts and discuss why the number of steps may be different for different family members (e.g., stride length). Simply by talking about physical activity, parents are showing children that they value physical activity.

▶ Pedometer Chore Time

Wearing a pedometer and monitoring steps while doing chores is another way to measure the amount of activity accumulated during lifestyle activity.

Purpose

1. To allow family members to monitor their physical activity levels while participating in chores
2. To add a sense of excitement to the normally dreaded "chore time"

Activity Description

1. Family members make a chart of family chores with a space for "steps taken" while doing the chores. See form 7.1 for an example of a family chores log.
2. Family members wear a pedometer while doing their chores.
3. Family members record the number of steps taken while completing the chore. This chart can be kept on the refrigerator and used for future reference. For example, a child may want to accumulate 300 more steps for the day but has to do a chore of his or her choice. The chart can help the child make an appropriate choice to meet his or her goal.
4. After all chores are finished, the family meets and discusses which chores are active and which are inactive. Also, they can brainstorm and create ways to increase the number of steps taken during relatively inactive chores.

▶ Errands With a Pedometer

Often families feel they are too busy to exercise because they are constantly running errands. Pedometers allow parents and children to see how much activity they can accumulate while completing errands. In a day of running to the grocery store, going to the mall, and driving to a soccer game, many steps can be accumulated.

Family Chores

Chore	_Mom_ steps	_Dad_ steps	_____ steps	_____ steps	Average steps

From *Pedometer Power: 67 Lessons for K–12* by Robert P. Pangrazi, Aaron Beighle, and Cara L. Sidman, 2003, Champaign, IL: Human Kinetics.

Purpose

1. To allow families to track the amount of activity they accumulate while running errands
2. To provide families with the information necessary to make lifestyle changes to increase daily physical activity

Activity Description

1. Family members wear a pedometer for several days while running errands.
2. Family members then record the total number of steps taken as well as the number of steps taken for each errand.
3. Calculations of the average number of steps taken by family members while running errands are completed.
4. The family should have a discussion about why one errand may have been more active than another. For example, driving to a soccer game may not allow for as many steps as a day walking at the mall.
5. The family can also discuss how the low activity days or errands could be changed to increase physical activity. For example, park at the far end of the parking lot, or take the steps instead of the elevator or escalator.

▶Pedometer Testing Different Physical Activities

Many favorite activities can be put to the test by the use of a pedometer. This test allows both parents and children to see the number of steps accumulated during their favorite activities (see figure 7.1 for some activity ideas).

Purpose

1. To test the steps accumulated from a variety of activities
2. To promote family activity

Activity Description

1. Each family member gets to pick an activity for family participation. The steps during that activity are recorded, thus testing the activity level.
2. The family keeps a chart of the activities they participate in and the corresponding steps for that activity. The list should be displayed on the refrigerator or in another prominent place in the home.

3. After each test, the family should discuss the level of the day's activity.

4. All family members can constantly seek new and enjoyable activities to test.

▶ Family Goals

Working together toward a common physical activity goal is a way for a family to promote lifestyle activity and show children that activity is valued in a household.

Purpose

1. To develop a number of activities that all family members can enjoy together

2. To work together toward a common physical activity goal

Activity Description

1. Create a log sheet (see form 7.2).

Form 7.2

Family Steps

Name	Day 1	Day 2	Day 3	Day 4	Individual total
Mom_____ steps					
Dad_____ steps					
_____ steps					
_____ steps					
_____ steps					
_____ steps					
_____ steps					
Daily total					
				Grand total	

From *Pedometer Power: 67 Lessons for K–12* by Robert P. Pangrazi, Aaron Beighle, and Cara L. Sidman, 2003, Champaign, IL: Human Kinetics.

2. Each family member wears the pedometer for 1 day.

3. After every family member has worn the pedometer for 1 day, they calculate their total number of steps.

4. The family sets a family goal based on this number. A 10 percent increase in total steps is a good start.

5. The family repeats items 2 and 3.

6. If the family owns or has access to one or two pedometers, each family member can wear the pedometer for 4 days. Weekend days are useful for showing how activity levels vary when family members aren't working or going to school.

▶ Family Dance Night

Because dancing is an enjoyable form of physical activity in which all family members can participate, a regular "family dance night" can be planned to increase step counts. This activity can be adapted to accommodate specific age levels and numbers of family members.

Purpose

1. To increase family activity by dancing to a variety of music

2. To develop and refine basic rhythmic movements in the nonthreatening family environment

Activity Description

1. Each family member (depending on age) chooses a song he or she wants to dance to during Dance Night.

2. Each family member is given a number, and one family member randomly selects the order of songs by the numbers. Each week, a different family member chooses the order.

3. Family Dance Night can be anything from a formal dance lesson taught by one of the children, as learned in physical education class, to an informal session in which everyone does their own thing to the preselected music.

4. The family should record pedometer step counts before and after the dance.

▶ Walk and Talk

Being able to talk with a friend while involved in physical activity increases the motivation for many students. Walking and talking is a good way for parents and youth to learn about each other without undue interference and distractions.

Purpose

1. To increase physical activity among family members
2. To increase communication among family members

Activity Description

1. Each family member is paired with another family member to take walks on specified days or evenings. A rotating list should be posted on the refrigerator, and every effort should be made to ensure that all family members have an opportunity to walk with each other at least once a week.
2. The family should develop a regular rotation for wearing pedometers, depending on the number of pedometers available to the family. For example, if the family has only one pedometer, both individuals in a walking pair should be given the chance to record their step counts on separate nights.
3. The walk should last at least 10 minutes, and each person should actively participate in a discussion (e.g., about their day, what's on their mind, how to increase their step counts).
4. One night a week, the entire family should walk and talk together as a whole.
5. The family should record pedometer step counts on a regular basis.

▶Walk Around the Clock

All people have different times during the day when they are most active or inactive. A reasonable goal is to try to be active at regular intervals throughout the day. This activity will help create awareness of activity patterns for youth and their parents.

Purpose

1. To increase awareness of physical activity levels throughout the day
2. To ultimately increase step counts

Activity Description

1. See form 7.3 for a sample chart to record step counts around the clock. Note the blanks provided to calculate total step counts at different segments of the day.

Form 7.3

Walk Around the Clock

Record your steps each hour.

Step Record

A.M.		P.M.	
5:00–6:00 A.M.	_____	12:00–1:00 P.M.	_____
6:00–7:00 A.M.	_____	1:00–2:00 P.M.	_____
7:00–8:00 A.M.	_____	2:00–3:00 P.M.	_____
8:00–9:00 A.M.	_____	3:00–4:00 P.M.	_____
9:00–10:00 A.M.	_____	4:00–5:00 P.M.	_____
10:00–11:00 A.M.	_____	5:00–6:00 P.M.	_____
11:00 A.M.–12:00 P.M.	_____	6:00–7:00 P.M.	_____
		7:00–8:00 P.M.	_____
		8:00–9:00 P.M.	_____

Morning steppers: (5:00 A.M.–12:00 P.M.)
Afternoon steppers: (12:00 P.M.–5:00 P.M.)
Eventing steppers: (5:00 P.M.–9:00 P.M.)
Total step count:

From *Pedometer Power: 67 Lessons for K–12* by Robert P. Pangrazi, Aaron Beighle, and Cara L. Sidman, 2003, Champaign, IL: Human Kinetics.

2. Family members can be labeled "morning steppers," "afternoon steppers," or "evening steppers" based on which part of the day they accumulate the greatest number of steps.

3. To increase step counts, the family should note which time of the day is the most inactive for each family member and discuss what can be done to make each family member more active (during those times, if possible).

▶Adopt-a-Neighborhood Street

This is a common civic duty activity that is done on highways throughout the United States. On a local basis, it is an excellent activity for youth and parents as they work together to keep neighborhood streets clean.

Purpose

1. To increase activity levels of family members
2. To develop family unity
3. To help the environment

Activity Description

1. Parents should adopt a neighborhood street in their area and the whole family should participate.
2. The family should record step counts after each street cleanup outing.

▶Family Scavenger Hunt

This is an enjoyable activity that is informal and easy to implement with families. Scavenger hunt items can be found around the house or the neighborhood if more activity is desired.

Purpose

1. To increase activity levels of family members
2. To promote teamwork and cooperation among family members (or neighborhoods)
3. To become educated about various topics related to health, wellness, and the environment

Activity Description

1. The family should select scavenger hunt teams of two or more.
2. Each team must have at least one pedometer.
3. See figure 7.2 for scavenger hunt items organized by category. The family should select as many items necessary to suit their (or their neighborhood's) needs. Gathering the items should promote physical activity as much as possible.
4. The team that returns with the most items and the highest step count is the winner.

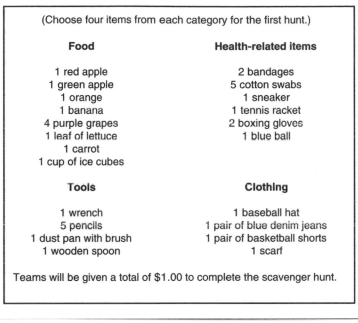

(Choose four items from each category for the first hunt.)

Food

1 red apple
1 green apple
1 orange
1 banana
4 purple grapes
1 leaf of lettuce
1 carrot
1 cup of ice cubes

Health-related items

2 bandages
5 cotton swabs
1 sneaker
1 tennis racket
2 boxing gloves
1 blue ball

Tools

1 wrench
5 pencils
1 dust pan with brush
1 wooden spoon

Clothing

1 baseball hat
1 pair of blue denim jeans
1 pair of basketball shorts
1 scarf

Teams will be given a total of $1.00 to complete the scavenger hunt.

Figure 7.2   Scavenger hunt items.

▶ *Season Stepping*

It is easy for the change in seasons to make a change in the activity levels of youth and adults. Learning to be active on a year-round basis is important in maintaining a healthy lifestyle.

Purpose

1. To enhance awareness of various obstacles to being physically active year-round.
2. To become more physically active during less active times of the year

Activity Description

See figure 7.3 for some ideas for increasing physical activity levels throughout the year as a family. Walking is one activity that can be done in any season.

▶ *Active Samaritans*

Teaching students to become productive members of society is important. What better way to do this than to encourage them to be active in

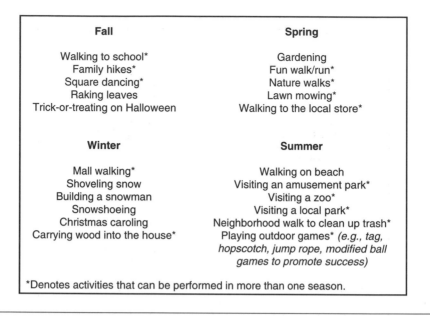

Fall	Spring
Walking to school*	Gardening
Family hikes*	Fun walk/run*
Square dancing*	Nature walks*
Raking leaves	Lawn mowing*
Trick-or-treating on Halloween	Walking to the local store*
Winter	**Summer**
Mall walking*	Walking on beach
Shoveling snow	Visiting an amusement park*
Building a snowman	Visiting a zoo*
Snowshoeing	Visiting a local park*
Christmas caroling	Neighborhood walk to clean up trash*
Carrying wood into the house*	Playing outdoor games* *(e.g., tag, hopscotch, jump rope, modified ball games to promote success)*

*Denotes activities that can be performed in more than one season.

Figure 7.3   Season stepping ideas for the family.

community services? In fact, many schools have community service clubs that volunteer for a variety of community service activities in their area. The following is a list of community service projects that incorporate the use of pedometers into the school activities.

1. Collect trash on the playground.
2. Rake leaves on the school property.
3. Rake leaves in the neighborhood on a Saturday and collect donations for a charity of the students' choice.
4. Participate in a local walkathon for the students' charity of choice in which donations are given per step.
5. Jump Rope for Heart or Play Hoops for Heart with donations based on the number of jumps or steps.

If You Want to Know More . . .

The following Web sites offer much more information about promoting physical activity in different ways that families can enjoy together.

Web Sites

www.valinet.com/~dbotkin
Daniel Botkin (professional footbagger, social worker, and coach) has put together an informative Web site that focuses on teaching and mentoring marginalized youth using sports, craft, and peer education—specifically using the popular, cooperative, and largely undiscovered sport of hacky sack, or footbag.

http://members.aol.com/acesday/aces.html
Project ACES (All Children Exercise Simultaneously). On one designated day each year (usually in May because it's National Physical Fitness and Sports Month), all school children will either exercise, walk, jog, bike, dance, do aerobics, or a combination of any of these activities for 15 to 45 minutes. Each school organizes its own participation assembly for the duration of the program. There is no specific routine to follow; just have the students do some form of exercise as close to the specified time as possible. Creativity is highly encouraged.

www.teelfamily.com/education/seasonal.html
This Web site provides activities for winter, spring, summer, and fall.

www.ymca.net
The Web site of the YMCA of the United States. It provides links to local YMCAs in your area.

www.americanheart.org/presenter.jhtml?identifier=2281
The Web site of American Heart Walk. Sponsored by the American Heart Association.

www.americanheart.org/presenter.jhtml?identifier=2360
The Web site of Jump Rope for Heart, an educational fund-raising event that teaches students the benefits of physical activity, how to keep their hearts healthy, and that they can help save lives in their own community.

www.nyshealthyschools.org/index.htm
The New York Statewide Center for Healthy Schools is a nationally recognized center dedicated to improving the health and educational achievement of students. The center recognizes the critical link between students' health and their ability to learn. Check out the Healthy Steps walking program.

www.beactivenc.org/about.html
This Web site provides information about how this organization is encouraging North Carolinians to create the policies, opportunities, facilities, and motivation to promote physical activity—and good health. In addition, you can participate in the Be Active steps program, which allows you to log the amount of steps you take (with a pedometer) on a daily basis, and kids can take some fun quizzes.

http://virginiadot.org/infoservice/prog-aah-default.asp
An example of an Adopt-a-Highway program in Virginia where volunteers supply the effort and the Department of Transportation supplies the equipment.

www.dot.ca.gov/hq/maint/adopt/coordinators.htm
California's Adopt-a-Highway program.

www.state.nj.us/dot/ops/adopt
New Jersey's Adopt-a-Highway program.

References

Brustad, R.J. 1993. Who will go out and play? Parental and psychological influences on children's attraction to physical activity. *Pediatr. Exerc. Sci.* 5:210–23.

—1996. Attraction to physical activity in urban schoolchildren: Parental socialization and gender influences. *Res. Q. Exercise Sport* 67:316–23.

Freedson, P.S. and S. Evenson. 1991. Familial aggregation in physical activity. *Res. Q. Exercise Sport* 62:384–89.

Kimiecik, J.C. and T.S. Horn. 1998. Parental beliefs and children's moderate-to-vigorous physical activity. *Res. Q. Exercise Sport* 69:163–75.

About the Authors

Dr. Robert P. Pangrazi is a well-respected physical education professor, researcher, and author. He is the author of 37 textbooks and more than 70 research and journal articles related to youth fitness and physical education. Dr. Pangrazi has been a keynote speaker for 29 state and district conventions and an invited speaker at nearly 200 conferences. He has presented in Canada, Sweden, Britain, Australia, and the Czech Republic. Dr. Pangrazi is a fellow of the American Academy of Kinesiology and Physical Education, an elected position limited to 125 members nationally. He also is an honor

Robert P. Pangrazi

fellow in the American Alliance for Health, Physical Education, Recreation and Dance.

Dr. Pangrazi lives in Tempe, Arizona, where he has been a professor in the department of kinesiology at Arizona State University since 1974. In his free time, Dr. Pangrazi enjoys walking, playing the piano, and reading.

A former physical education teacher, **Aaron Beighle** has broad experience conducting research with children who use pedometers and working with teachers who implement pedometers in schools. A member of the American Alliance for Health, Physical Education, Recreation and Dance (AAHPERD), the National Association for Sport and Physical Education (NASPE), and the National Association for Physical Education in Higher Education (NAPEHE), he is currently pursuing his doctoral degree at Arizona State University, where he is a graduate teaching assistant and student teaching supervisor in the department of kinesiology. Aaron

Aaron Beighle

enjoys spending time with his wife, Barbara, and family, as well as traveling and participating in a wide variety of physical activities. He resides in Mesa, Arizona.

Dr. Cara L. Sidman holds a PhD in exercise and wellness, for which she prepared a dissertation on using pedometers to promote physical activity. She also has published an article on pedometers in the *ACSM Health & Fitness Journal.* A member of AAPHERD and an alliance member of ACSM, Cara is an assistant professor in the School of Kinesiology and Recreation Studies at James Madison University in Harrisonburg, Virginia, where she resides. In her leisure time, she enjoys hiking, jogging, and reading.

Cara L. Sidman